The Films of
Laurence
OLIVIER

by MARGARET MORLEY

With images by DILYS POWELL, ROGER MANVELL,
SHERIDAN MORLEY and TOM HUTCHINSON

The Films of
Laurence
OLIVIER

by MARGARET MORLEY

*With images by DILYS POWELL, ROGER MANVELL,
SHERIDAN MORLEY and TOM HUTCHINSON*

and a foreword by
MICHAEL CAINE

The Citadel Press   Secaucus, N.J.

FOREWORD

BY MICHAEL CAINE

When I was originally offered my rôle in *Sleuth* opposite Laurence Olivier, apart from feeling slightly nervous, my first thought was "What am I going to call him?" He is the only actor ever to have been made a Lord. The next day I received a letter from Lord Olivier saying, amongst other things, that from the moment we met (which was for the first time) I must call him Larry. I think it is typical of the man that he had already started sorting out the difficulties of making the film and he had come across one of mine and wiped it out immediately.

My nervous reaction to working with him was not only out of respect for his talent, which is tremendous, but also because I knew from my own theatre experience that sometimes these theatrical giants are given to riding roughshod over some of the other members of the cast. I faced the first day with some trepidation. My worries proved to be unfounded as Larry turned out to be one of the most friendly and helpful actors I have ever worked with.

That he is a professional goes without saying, but the degree of professionalism is extraordinary and exhausting. Throughout the film he would come charging into my room to rehearse again and again, and to try new things until together we had milked the scene of every value it had.

To act with Laurence Olivier is rather like skating with Sonja Henie. The fact that you can do it is not necessarily going to do you much good. His command of his art is complete. This much you can see as an observer but it is not until you actually work with him that you experience what I used to call during the filming of *Sleuth* the 'take off'. This is a phenomenon which seems to overcome him when, instead of just being brilliant which is something that another artist can at least try to keep up with, he will suddenly leap into a realm of acting where it is virtually impossible to follow. I knew that he could do this in the theatre, but it is much more difficult to do this in films. He has managed to master both mediums.

I think that he would have had a really great film career, but he chose to concentrate on the theatre which was a great loss to the cinema; even bearing that in mind, you can see from this book that his film contribution is still tremendous. Can you imagine what he would have done had he concentrated?

My foreword has been a paean of praise. This does not mean that he does not make mistakes, but that when he does he has enough humility to ask for another 'take' and to thank you for helping him to get it right.

"It was a privilege, Larry".

10

OLIVIER: THE CAREER

BY MARGARET MORLEY

"Between good and great acting is fixed an inexorable gulf which may be crossed only by the elect, whose visas are in order: Laurence Olivier pole-vaults over it, hair-raisingly, in a single animal leap. Great acting comes more easily to him than to any of his colleagues".

Thus Kenneth Tynan (Olivier's one-time National Theatre adviser and for twenty years his most constant chronicler) pinpoints the animal instinct for danger and survival which has always been at the root of the Olivier talent.

"He looks like a man who could lynch a crowd" said another critic, while a director who worked frequently with him added "Olivier is like a panther — just when you think you know where he is and that you've got him cornered, he springs out at you from some totally different direction".

It's hard to think of a better definition of Olivier on the screen: the winner of two Academy Awards and another half-dozen nominations, director and star of the three most successful Shakespeare films ever made, and veteran of nearly half a hundred other movies remains at seventy the least predictable of all our actors.

He was the first one ever to get a peerage, and the founder-director of the National Theatre, which in itself might suggest a film career inevitably either incidental or secondary. Yet Spencer Tracy reckoned that Olivier's films made him "the greatest of them all" and Tracy was in a position to know, since he was there cheerfully giving away a title which he could justifiably have kept for himself.

Three marriages, four children, fifty years in the business and (in the past decade) three severe illnesses add up to a not exactly uneventful life, but Olivier shows no fundamental sign of weakening or giving up just yet: as the National Theatre passed into other hands and the British film industry showed all the symptoms of final collapse he moved in the mid-1970s to television, becoming executive producer and sometimes also director and star of a whole series of Granada classics. Why? "Because it was a such a wonderful opportunity to carry on: I don't always like myself as I am, and if I hadn't been able to become an actor I'd have been in despair. But you get a chance, if you're an actor, to be somebody else . . . an awful lot of am-

bition can be sublimated in acting.

"If ever I wanted to be a Duke, I've played a Duke: if I've ever wanted to be Archbishop of Canterbury, I've played that too. I've played Kings and Generals and sometimes, when I've felt miserable, I've been able to look forward to being Coriolanus or Archie Rice or anyone but me. And that's a wonderful feeling".

The acknowledged leading actor of the English-speaking stage was born on May 22, 1907 at Dorking in Surrey. He began his career at the age of nine playing Brutus in a school play. The critics were not out in force for this event but Dame Sybil Thorndike (a family friend and like Olivier a clergyman's child) was there with her husband

Stratford-on-Avon, 1922: as Katharina in a schoolboy *Taming of the Shrew*.

Lewis Casson, and they both pronounced the boy "a born actor".

His father, an Anglican vicar, and from all accounts one given to dramatic sermons, actively encouraged the idea of his younger son going on the stage. After attending the choir school attached to All Saints Church in London, Olivier went on to St. Edward's School in Oxford and his next recorded performance was a month before his fourteenth birthday when he played Katharina in *The Taming of the Shrew* at the Stratford Shakespeare Festival in a special boys' performance.

Having finished at St. Edward's, Olivier wondered if he should join his brother on a rubber plantation in India, but his father told him in no uncertain terms what he expected of his son. So Laurence Olivier went to the Central School and studied under Elsie Fogerty. He then had nearly ten years' stage experience, notably with the Birmingham Repertory Company, before going into films in 1930.

A very experienced stage actor by this time, he did not begin films as a bit player — no walk-ons or crowd scenes but instead leading parts, although the films themselves were not at the outset extremely distinguished. He was the juvenile lead, the veritably handsome, nay beautiful young man, even though he considered himself to be a miserably thin, scraggly creature and always padded the calves of his tights before appearing on stage in them.

Olivier first went to America professionally in August, 1929 to play Hugh Bromilow in *Murder on the Second Floor* at the Eltinge Theatre. It was not a success but his next visit to New York as Victor Prynne in Noel Coward's *Private Lives* did him considerably more good. His first wife, Jill Esmond, to whom he had proposed after a three-week courtship, was also in the cast of five.

Olivier had worried about the part of Victor — it was not a very large one, but Coward convinced him that he should appear in a success for a change and Olivier still credits Coward as one of the major influences on his life and acting.

It was during the New York run of *Private Lives* that Hollywood discovered Olivier for the first time. He and Jill Esmond made screen tests for MGM and Paramount before signing with RKO but the early films they made were startling neither in themselves nor in their impact, and Olivier went back to England to make *Perfect Understanding* with Gloria Swanson for her own company.

Then came the disastrous *Queen Christina*, back in Hollywood — disastrous for Olivier, who was cast as Greta Garbo's lover when neither Leslie Howard nor Ronald Colman were available, only to be re-

placed after a few days shooting by John Gilbert. Some versions of the story say he was replaced because Garbo wanted to do Gilbert a good turn, but Olivier himself has said he just was not adequate in the part.

Between the time Olivier reached the London stage in 1928 and 1935 when he signed with Alexander Korda he had chalked up seventeen plays, but the number itself is indicative of the fact that few of them were long-running box-office successes. For Korda he first became involved in what was projected as a massive documentary about man's attempt to fly. It was called *Conquest of the Air* and ran into innumerable production and economic problems; it wasn't until 1940 that a truncated version of it was finally released. Olivier played Lunardi, the balloonist, and it could be looked upon as the first of those character cameos he came to perfect 25 years later.

Then, in 1935, Olivier had an enormous stage success in *Romeo and Juliet* at the New Theatre in London. He and John Gielgud alternated the rôles of Romeo and Mercutio to constant praise from the critics. This led to his screen casting opposite

the German star, Elizabeth Bergner, in *As You Like It*: his first foray into screen Shakespeare was a personal success, though the film itself had a mixed reception.

It was in January 1937 that he joined the Old Vic company and began to find his form as a stage actor playing the great classical parts: Hamlet, Henry V, and Macbeth. In films he was still the attractive young romantic hero, in one film swashbuckling, in another a naïve young lawyer and in another just tear-jerking. It was during the filming of the swashbuckler, *Fire Over England*, that he and his co-star Vivien Leigh (who were daily in each other's company) fell in love.

Late in 1938 Olivier returned to Hollywood, with great reluctance, to film *Wuthering Heights*. By now clearly successful on stage, he still had good reason on past form not to trust his luck in films. But he had not reckoned with the director William Wyler, who worked him hard and long and managed to convince him that film acting had very little to do with what he had been trained for theatrically. At first Olivier fought him, but gradually he began to understand and respond — and

the resulting Heathcliff was a brilliant interpretation of Emily Brontë's dark mysterious character which brought Olivier's first Academy Award nomination.

After *Wuthering Heights*, he went back to Broadway to play Gaylord Easterbrook in *No Time For Comedy* and when he returned to Hollywood and Hitchcock's *Rebecca* it was with less trepidation. Olivier gave a classic performance as the introspective Max de Winter, received another nomination as best actor and followed that with the aristocratic Darcy in Jane Austen's *Pride and Prejudice*. He then had a rare failure on the Broadway stage where he directed himself and Vivien Leigh in a disastrous production of *Romeo and Juliet*. Much of the money in the production was his own and he lost it.

England was by now at war. In Hollywood, Olivier and Leigh, just married, made *Lady Hamilton* for Alexander Korda. It was hoped that the tale of the famous war hero and his Emma, acted by the extremely famous team, would help to sway America into the war. Its influence was rather less, though it did become Winston Churchill's favourite film.

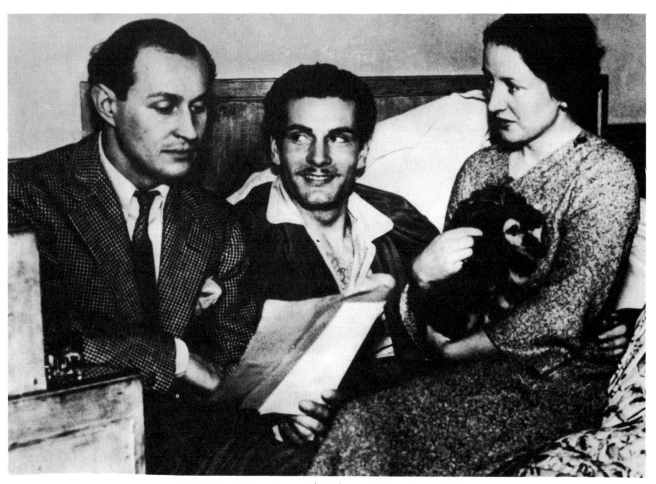

With Robert Douglas and Jill Esmond, December 1934

13

Olivier was in great demand: just about every studio in Hollywood had a film for him. One studio even offered to delay *How Green Was My Valley* until he could get around to it. Returning to England, he joined the Royal Navy Fleet Air Arm and served from 1940 to 1944, although he was released on two occasions to play guest roles in propaganda films.

In *49th Parallel*, an all-star and very successful effort commissioned by the Ministry of Information, he played a French-Canadian trapper. His accent was Russian in the other film, *The Demi-Paradise*.

In 1944 he went back to the Old Vic Company where he played the Button-Moulder in *Peer Gynt*, the hunchbacked King in *Richard III* and Astrov in *Uncle Vanya*. This was also the year of *Henry V*, Olivier's first, albeit reluctant, attempt at directing for the screen. He wanted to make the film as a firm and heroic statement of British patriotism and Filippo de Giudice put up the money, but Olivier could not find a director. Perhaps too many were wary of Shakespeare on film — it had never really worked. Olivier asked William Wyler who in effect said 'do it yourself' — so he did, and received for it a special Academy Award for outstanding achievement as an actor, producer and director.

He was appointed co-director of the Old Vic company and continued playing the classic stage rôles — Oedipus, Hotspur, Lear. After the war, the Old Vic travelled to the Comédie Française and in 1947 Olivier finally came back to films: this time it was again Shakespeare and again he directed. During the filming of *Hamlet* he received his knighthood in the Birthday Honours. After *Hamlet*, the Old Vic company went on an extended tour of Australia.

Back in London, he and Vivien Leigh continued to reign both professionally and socially: on stage Vivien Leigh was Cleopatra while Olivier was Shaw's Caesar and Shakespeare's Antony. Then in 1952, when his wife wanted to make a film in Hollywood, he accepted the part of George Hurstwood in *Carrie*, so that they would not have to face separation. Despite the film's box-office failure his was for many critics a welcome return to the American cinema.

But, for Sir Laurence, highly acclaimed as a stage actor, a film star, a director in both media and the man who had succeeded where all others had failed in bringing Shakespeare to the screen, what was there left to try? He had never sung on screen, so he did that in *The Beggar's Opera*, for Peter Brook. The critics were undecided about his Macheath and the audiences stayed away in thousands. In 1955 he went back to Shakespeare on film and immor-

With his then wife Vivien Leigh, July 1955.

talised his stage portrayal of the hunchback *Richard III*, netting himself a second Shakespearean Oscar in the process. He then tried unsuccessfully to raise the capital for a film of *Macbeth*, a project he had long had in mind and which was destined to remain only in his mind.

In 1957, the same year as he received an Honorary D.Litt. from Oxford University, he surprised the London theatrical scene by playing Archie Rice in John Osborne's *The Entertainer* for the English Stage Company at the Royal Court Theatre. Here was England's greatest classical actor playing a seedy music hall comedian in a play by the angriest of the young men. Doom and disaster were predicted and its enormous success was, to say the least, unexpected.

He then toured Europe with the more predictable *Titus Andronicus* before coming back and transferring *The Entertainer* to the Palace Theatre for an extended run.

Marilyn Monroe arrived in England in 1957 to be directed by Olivier for her own company in *The*

With Joan Plowright in *The Entertainer*, 1957.

Prince and the Showgirl: he himself played the part of the Duke, a character role he had created on stage and a gentle parody of the romantic heroes of his early career. It was, from all reports, a fairly stormy set, but he extracted a marvellous performance from Monroe before going back to concentrating on his own performance in *The Devil's Disciple*. In 1960 he made the film of *The Entertainer* and earned his first X certificate as well as another Academy Award nomination.

Despite the considerable commercial success he was now having in his film career, the stage was never far away and in 1961 he was appointed Director of the Chichester Festival Theatre. This was also the year he entered the world of epics in *Spartacus*, and married Joan Plowright who had played his daughter in *The Entertainer*.

As director of the Festival Theatre he presented a varied selection of plays and organised the general running of the theatre with great success, thus paving the way for his next appointment. With the creation of the National Theatre of Great Britain in

1963 he was the logical choice for its first Director. During his period at the National, his film career became diffuse: there were the films he made for the money to support himself and his new young family so he could continue with the less well-paid life of the theatre, and there were the films which were in fact no more than recorded versions of stage successes. There were also one or two he made because he actually wanted to make them on their own merits as screenplays.

But in 1973, Laurence Olivier returned to real films with a vengeance: his duties at the National Theatre now finished, he took on the enormously taxing part of Andrew Wyke in *Sleuth*, earning himself yet another Academy Award nomination — an almost routine process, now, for him though he has yet to add a third to the couple of Oscars he actually carried off for *Henry V* and *Hamlet*.

Then, following a period of severe illness which would have finished many less resilient careers, there came three more guest shots and one more major rôle (in Schlesinger's *Marathon Man*) as well as an entire Granada Television series of popular classics for which he was often both producer and star.

At the time of writing (mid-1977) Olivier has appeared in a total of 49 films in 46 years: not an unimpressive total for a man who once said that films were something an actor should do when he wasn't required in the theatre.

What of the future? "As long as I can stand", Olivier has said, "I'll go on doing my job", and even after a decade in which his physical and mental resources have been tested to the uttermost it remains impossible to think of him in absolute or total retirement. Joan Plowright, his third wife and the mother of his three younger children (there is an elder son by Jill Esmond) said once that she somehow could not visualise her husband in an orchard working on his memoirs, and he added that he knew of no greater pleasure in life than setting off to work each morning and looking back over his shoulder to see the children waving from the window.

Other men on the verge of their seventieth birthdays might have talked of the pleasures of returning home; but then Olivier is not other men.

With his first wife Jill Esmond, arriving at the wedding of their son Tarquin.

With Joan Plowright, 1973, to receive his Best Actor award from The Evening Standard

With Joan Plowright, celebrating the announcement of his peerage, June 1976.

OLIVIER: THE PREWAR YEARS

BY DILYS POWELL

It is comparatively easy to recognise the embryo exponent of *personality*: a Bogart, given half a chance, will stand out from the screen. The *actor* presents a more difficult problem, and perhaps one may be excused for failing to see in the smooth young Straker of *Potiphar's Wife* the passionate, complex figure of a future Heathcliff.

Laurence Olivier was a star on the stage long before he was regarded with much seriousness in the cinema. He was playing the great roles in high company — *Hamlet* at the Old Vic, *Hamlet* at Elsinore; there was a *Macbeth* in 1937, there was an *Iago*: neither, or so I thought at the time, with great depth, but the promise was clearly there. Nevertheless early in his career he was already active on the screen.

By the end of the nineteen-twenties the cinema was no longer silent. It had not learned, however, to cultivate its own voices. The splendid figures of the silent screen too often spoke in raven tones; and everywhere stage-trained players were in demand. The young Olivier was soon busy.

In 1930 — it was the year in which he played in Noël Coward's *Private Lives* on the London stage — he appeared in a short comedy called *Too Many Crooks*; in the same year he moved to a more ambitious rôle in *The Temporary Widow*. A year later came *Potiphar's Wife*; in 1933 *Perfect Understanding* and *No Funny Business*. These films of the beginning of the nineteen-thirties may be preserved in archives. In memory they have small place; living much abroad and not yet working as a professional critic, I at the time saw none of them, and such acquaintance as I have was to come later.

Probably they are representative enough of the British cinema of the period. It was nondescript, but it was struggling. Battling to assert itself against the domination of Hollywood, it was importing glamorous names from across the Atlantic; Gloria Swanson was the heroine of *Perfect Understanding* (in which Olivier played an errant husband). Alexander Korda was making audacious plans, and the first great Korda surprise came in 1932 with *The Private Life of Henry VIII*. Olivier was not drawn in until

1935, when in *Moscow Nights* he worked with a director who was himself in the early stages of a distinguished career — Anthony Asquith. But all the time the young actor was doing what long afterwards in John Osborne's *The Entertainer* he would claim to be doing: having a go.

He worked in the American as well as the British cinema. *Friends and Lovers* (1931), with Adolphe Menjou and Stroheim in the cast, was made in the United States; so was *Westward Passage* (1932); so was *The Yellow Ticket*, a melodrama which still,

after forty-three years, can be watched with interest. It was, after all, directed by the famous Raoul Walsh, destined to become one of Hollywood's Old Reliables and indeed something of a cult figure. An adaptation of a stage melodrama about Czarist Russia, it is a film which moves with notable dash. But one cannot give Olivier much credit for its success; as the English journalist who rescues the beautiful Jewess from the iniquities, not to say the lecheries, of the Russian police he plays with no more than conventional smoothness. Possibly he was not encouraged to do more: Walsh's gifts, and they are considerable, have always been for action rather than character. If one had not known of Olivier's achievements in the theatre one might have expected him to settle down in Hollywood as a second string, one of those bright young men who learn something of the fluency of the American screen, make a brief foray into the gossip columns, the headlines and the world of promise, then sink back into the ranks of the supporting players. One can think of a dozen actors of the sort, presentable, competent, but lacking drive, distinction, the will to survive.

British stage celebrities of the period often found difficulty in getting the hang of working to the camera instead of to an audience. Charles Laughton was among those quick to grasp the subtleties of playing for the screen, but there were famous figures who took years to accept the differences of size and volume, gesture and emphasis, and to understand the qualities of cursiveness and relaxation demanded by the new medium. Perhaps the cinema for its part failed to understand the possibilities of the stage performer; players of reputation and talent were often woefully miscast and misused. But one cannot say quite that of Olivier; he was at least given an opening — though it may not always have been the right one.

Today stage and film stars change their setting with ease; everybody — well, nearly everybody — has learned the dual techniques and styles. But in the nineteen-thirties British players, though they had not been strait-jacketed into the traditions of declamation of, say, the Comédie Française, nevertheless had, many of them, a classical style to escape from. And something else: it is a mistake to assume that all the great luminaries of Hollywood belonged from the start to the screen. Spencer Tracy had stage beginnings. Humphrey Bogart played Duke Mantee on the stage before his appearance in the film version of *The Petrified Forest* made him a star. All the same there was a difference between the British and the American approach. In America a man took no RADA courses. There was no Strasberg school yet to teach him Method acting. He might drift into

With Elissa Landi, in *The Yellow Passport* (1931).

films. A good horseman might turn into a Gary Cooper or a John Wayne. Some quirk of voice, some angle of mouth or nose or eyes might signal a screen personality. And the lucky fellow had no traditions to overcome. He learned the business of film acting from the ground up.

In Britain the list of film players included none of the ex-sodajerks one finds in the biographies, romanticised no doubt, of the Hollywood stars; Laurence Olivier never graduated as an elephant-trainer. Actors and actresses worked for films when they could; the demarcation between screen players and theatre players which came to be generally accepted in the United States hardly existed in the Britain of the decade before the Second World War. It would be a long time before this country would foster its own film stars, and even today the economics of the business make it difficult for more than a handful of players, most of them anyway enjoying international connections, to devote themselves entirely to the cinema. Obviously Laurence Olivier would never join that small group; his life was from the start too deeply rooted in the theatre. Presently, however, he would learn mastery of that pitiless observer, the camera. But not in his own country. In the British cinema he was the light romantic in

the light comedy, the young man in the unfriendly law courts; he was the juvenile lead. He would have to learn somewhere else.

Looking today at *Potiphar's Wife* one sees a party of British stage players trapped in birdlime; they struggle. One or two have a shot at character-types; but the gestures are self-conscious and the dramatic pauses distressingly exaggerated. For Olivier as the chauffeur falsely accused of assault one can say little more than that he does not over-act. In the dock he looks positively unconcerned, though it is true that with his nineteen-thirties hairline moustache and spruce figure he might indeed be some rich woman's driver. At least he does not shift out of type. Curious how small he looks; nothing except that faint hollowing of the cheeks to suggest the powerful charm of the actor of the future. Perhaps the literary elements in his dramatic beginnings made him feel he hadn't much to work on, and indeed he hadn't. He has to remain silent throughout the trial scene in *Potiphar's Wife*. When he is given lines they are embarrassing: detaching himself from an embrace itself far from passionate, "So you just want me," he says to the woman bent on seducing him, "as a plaything!" One would see a performance of a very different order when five years later he

21

With Ann Harding in *Westward Passage* (1932).

appeared in the film version of *As You Like It*.
But that, with the Shakespearean lines to support
him, was not the best test of Olivier as a film actor.
Fire Over England, at roughly the same date, gave
one a better chance to judge.

A tale of England threatened by the Armada
(Clemence Dane had a hand in the script), it very
properly gave the grand historical phrases to Queen
Elizabeth, who was played by Flora Robson; Olivier
as a fictitious character was left doing what he could
with some decent but uninspiring expressions of
love, patriotism, royalist fervour and filial devotion.
Freed from the law courts ambiance (not to men-
tion the moustache) of earlier films, he presented a
pleasing romantic figure, handsome, acrobatic, leap-
ing from balconies and riding off in all directions.
As an English secret agent at the Spanish court he
showed a gift for self-disguise; once or twice one
could hear in the voice that flute-note which later
he would strengthen and use to such effect. He
looked, he sounded like a hero-player with a future.
But he did not look like a major film actor.

There were still one or two essays in the young-
man-about-town manner to be seen, still one or
two left-overs from the conventional, uncommitted
style to be forgotten. I remember seeing in 1939
both *Twenty-One Days* and the spy film *Q Planes*
and being surprised that the actor made so slight an
impression; he was still, in those two modest British
pieces, dashing but undistinguished. I was surprised
because a turning-point had already been reached.
We had already seen *Wuthering Heights*. And the
transformation had been effected not in England
but in the United States, where for the first time
Olivier had been working with an important American director at the height of his powers.

William Wyler had experience, reputation, authority;
he lived with the cinema. He taught the Englishman
a proper respect for the medium; he taught him
not to act but to think cinema. Olivier has acknowledged his debt, as well he might; for *Wuthering
Heights* saw his metamorphosis from a lightweight
romantic to a figure of passion and rage. His Heathcliff grew from a savage adoring boy to a man
obsessed by jealous love; scarcely possible to believe
that this was the player one had watched in *Potiphar's Wife* or even *Fire Over England*. There were
unforgettable moments — the despairing words, for
instance, at Cathy's bedside: "do not leave me," he
cries as the curtains in the room of death stir with
the wind from the moors, "do not leave me in this
abyss where I cannot find you!" The script preserves
fragments of the Brontë dialogue; they sustain the
actor; and one should remember in judging the per-

With Jill Esmond in *No Funny Business* (1933).

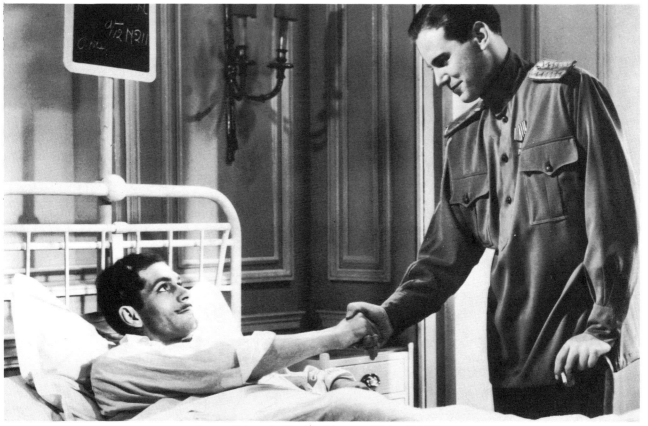

Ignatoff, hospitalised in *Moscow Nights* (1935).

formance that with the exception of *As You Like It* this was the first film in which he had been allowed to speak in reasonably literate terms.

But it was not the vocal delivery, fine though that was, which marked his transformation. The face, the gesture of the body, everything in the passages after Heathcliff's return to find Cathy married had command, and a command which went beyond the romantic. The cinema was not yet of an age to admit the demonic in Emily Brontë's hero. But Olivier — and Wyler — went as far as was practicable in the Hollywood of the late nineteen-thirties. One doesn't easily forget the look of cold dislike which this Heathcliff turns on the wife he has taken as an instrument of revenge.

After *Wuthering Heights* one might have expected *Jane Eyre* and Rochester; that went to Orson Welles. But there was *Rebecca* and the darkling figure of Max de Winter, another man haunted, though in a different fashion, by the memory of a woman. Olivier was not the first choice. Ronald Colman, had he been available, would have been picked by the tycoon-producer David O. Selznick; William Powell was in the running; Hollywood, like the rest of us, has lunatic moments. But this Englishman got the job.

Rebecca was the first film to be directed by Hitchcock in the United States. Not my least but among my less favourite Hitchcocks, it seems to me weighed down by the size of its setting; perhaps the weight oppressed the actor himself. Or possibly traces of stage technique still lingered; at any rate Selznick sent one of his famous memoranda complaining to the director that the speech was too fast and the reactions too slow "as if he were deciding whether or not to run for President instead of whether or not to give a ball". Hitchcock, interested in players as instruments of narrative rather than as illuminators of characters, in his published talks with Truffaut says nothing about the actor. But presumably the speeding up was successful, for the performance is perfectly timed.

In the series of romantic portraits which engaged Olivier up to the early days of the war it is not the most interesting. It was in any case designed from the start to be subordinate to the portrait of the girl whom the character marries and bewilders by his black moods. Selznick had hesitated anxiously and long before he picked Joan Fontaine; he had hoped to repeat his success in choosing as the Scarlett O'Hara of *Gone With the Wind* one of the less starry candidates. But subordinate or no, the sense of power was there in this Max de Winter: formidable charm allied to a saturnine melancholy.

Perhaps Olivier was in danger of repeating himself. With Heathcliff he had broken away from conventional heroics. With Max de Winter, mysterious, aloof, he had not yet won the right to break away from brooding.

In *Pride and Prejudice*, the film which followed *Rebecca*, the aloofness was of a different kind: class aloofness. Class is a national affair. English class, French class, American class — each has its own rules; it would be difficult for an American actor to bring to the role of Darcy the peculiar snobbishness of Jane Austen's English gentleman. Olivier, son of an English clergyman, knew class in his bones, and from this version of the novel (Aldous Huxley was co-author of a script based on the stage dramatisation) one recalls, apart from a few minor vulgarisms and anachronisms, the elegant manners both of Elizabeth Bennet, played by Greer Garson, and of the fastidious Darcy.

By now, like other British actors working in Hollywood, Olivier felt the need to get back to an England at war, but his next film, though a British production, *Lady Hamilton*, was made in Hollywood, away from the war. It was directed by Alexander Korda, who at this time was casting him fairly regularly; not only *Moscow Nights* but *Twenty-One Days*, *Q Planes*, *The Divorce of Lady X* and *Conquest of the Air* (a documentary about the history of flying) were Korda productions. This time Vivien Leigh, who had been disappointed by her rejection for the role in *Rebecca*, played opposite the Nelson of Olivier. In theory it was an auspicious choice. In practice, though one could always rely on the actor's equipment for the heroic roles (there was a kind of splendour in the death-scene) the romantic and the historical elements in the story never fused. Come to that, I cannot think of a successful Nelson film; none of the attempts which I have seen has achieved a proper balance. And Korda was a man with ideas rather than a good director.

Lady Hamilton appeared in 1941. Once threatened by Napoleon, now England was threatened by Hitler; the historical parallel was seductive, and it certainly seduced Churchill, who repeatedly asked for private showings of the film and, so one heard, saw it through tears. And one can understand the emotions stirred in the Churchillian sense of destiny. But for many of us *Lady Hamilton* seemed conventional in romance and perfunctory in history; the love-story thinned into propaganda. Perhaps Vivien Leigh was too slight a partner. At any rate the obsessive quality of the relationship was lost. Olivier was still not abandoning the role of the romantic hero. He was still not extending the range of character.

But with *49th Parallel* there was a change. Made partly in Britain and partly in Canada, it had the benefit of a director, Michael Powell, endowed with a talent at the time rare among British film-makers. Though fiction, the film, an episodic adventure, was made with the backing of the Ministry of Information; it had the intentions of propaganda, and it did not single out as star any name from a cast of distinguished players, among them Leslie Howard, Raymond Massey and Anton Walbrook.

Laurence Olivier appeared in one episode in the story of the six Nazis trying, after the destruction of their submarine, to escape across Canada to a United States still neutral. He played the French trapper in an Eskimo village: a man confronted by an evil outside his knowledge and his comprehension. The figure was not obviously heroic — no eloquence, no dramatic gestures, the speech hesitant in its French-English accent, everything gentle, quiet, slow. One saw a player who, breaking away from the grand romantic manner, had accepted the business of an actor to create an image of life not out of his personality but out of his experience and his imagination.

His next film showed that the change was radical.

Today the theme of *The Demi-Paradise* might well seem extravagantly indulgent to British character. Few of us would claim that the nation of eccentrics and xenophobes (domestic pets themselves had to be snatched away from the contagion of a foreigner) presented at the start of the film could be converted, even by a world conflagration, into a society of Cheeryble Brothers and Sisters. But in the story of

the young Russian engineer who, after a chill prewar reception, returns when Russia has entered the war to find a changed Britain two things make an audience swallow the flattery. One was the direction by Anthony Asquith, now for the second time working with Olivier. A man totally without malice, Asquith had an eye delighted by the absurd; with him satire — and the first half of the film is a satire on British insularity — was always rooted in affection. He was the most loving of directors; and something of his feeling affected his cast.

At any rate the other element which made the myth of a national regeneration acceptable was the performance of Olivier himself. Once again there was the modesty and simplicity which one saw in the French trapper of *49th Parallel*. But this time there was room for the character, as it were, to flow, to react, hesitate, be puzzled by the vagaries of an alien society, at last to warm to the warmth released by a shared danger. Anybody who ever met Asquith in a Russian setting — I remember him at a Moscow Festival — will testify to his passionate desire for Anglo-Russian understanding. The fantasy of *The Demi-Paradise* was something more than propaganda; it grew out of hope. And Olivier was there to interpret the fantasy, to give it a human face.

He brought to the film his heartbreaking charm. But he brought far more. The handsome romantic hero had effaced himself. In his place the great actor was emerging.

With Ralph Richardson in *Q Planes* (1939).

Shylock in Jonathan Miller's *The Merchant of Venice* (1972).

OLIVIER: THE SHAKESPEARIAN

BY ROGER MANVELL

Laurence Olivier, a pioneer in many aspects of stage production and the interpretation of character in the 20th century theatre, was also to be a pioneer in film-making. As a director, his work has been restricted to films adapted from Shakespeare's plays — *Henry V* (1944), *Hamlet* (1948), *Richard III* (1955), in all of which he also played the leading parts. In addition, he has acted in three films adapted from Shakespeare which span almost forty years — *As You Like It* (1936), *Othello* (1965) and *The Merchant of Venice* (1972).

Olivier was the first director of film to come to terms with the essential problems which face anyone adapting Shakespeare's plays for the screen. Shakespeare, for all the academic scaffolding which virtually hides the plays as working scripts for the theatre or enshrines them as holy writ, was a popular dramatist who wanted his work to be successful at the Elizabethan and Jacobean box-office. As indeed it was. His plays are vigorously plotted, and (since they are all free of copyright protection) formed the story-basis for some 400 silent films, made primarily in America, Britain and Germany. But no one would pretend that these did more than sketch the story-outline of the plays in crude mime, though one or two have genuine interest for the theatre historian — the record in 1911 of scenes from Frank Benson's production at Stratford-upon-Avon, and the far more ambitious version of Johnston Forbes-Robertson's *Hamlet* (1913) running feature-length, with extracts from the speeches appearing as captions inset between scenes of the actors' elaborate miming. There was also an interesting version of *Othello* starring Emil Jannings and made, with much melodramatic gesture, in Germany in 1922. But Shakespeare and the film could not unite in any proper sense until the establishment of sound on film in the late 1920s.

At once the producers became shy of Shakespeare. Sound films were cumbersome and expensive to make in the early 1930s. Shakespeare's language was a deterrent; the popular audience simply would not understand it. The cinema was in any case fighting for its life in a period of acute economic depression. So the 15-year period between the coming of sound and Laurence Olivier's *Henry V* saw the production of only four notable Shakespearian films, *The Taming of the Shrew* (1929), *A Midsummer Night's Dream* (1935), *Romeo and Juliet* (1936) and *As You Like It* (1936), all of which Olivier was to realise were in many respects unsatisfactory.

Shakespeare at first sight seems eminently adaptable to the screen. Even his greatest plays have the form and movement of high melodrama in exotic settings, while his comedies have immediate charm with their colourful love stories of lords and ladies moving in splendid courts and magic woodlands. Moreover, they have the structure and continuity of film-scripts — *Macbeth* (for example) running through 25 changes of scene on battlefields, barren heaths, outside and inside castles, in varied environments of Scotland and England. *Antony and Cleopatra* has no less than 42 changes of scene, covering places as various as Alexandria, Rome, Messina, Misenum, Syria, Athens and Actium, to say nothing of battle actions on land and sea; in other words, it is the very epitome of a screen epic. All this, together with the fame of the author as world dramatist extraordinary, offer lasting temptation to producers who can take it all for nothing in an industry where story 'properties' (as distinct from their script adaptations) can cost tens or even hundreds of thousands of dollars in film rights.

But although Shakespeare has his appeal in the studios, producers in the 1930s fought shy of his language, and adopted the simplest way out they knew — *cut*. Cut anything that would not easily be understood. Cut anything that did not directly forward the plot or offer immediate excitement as part of character conflict. In fact, cut anything that did not relate to action or to relationships the film directors and their actors could make visually interesting.

The film had been established since the silent days as a visual medium (when it could not be anything else), achieving all its effects through action played in shots which followed each other in dynamic progression or with a cumulative build-up of highly-charged atmosphere. Shakespeare's lengthy speeches simply had to be cut or drastically pruned. Nevertheless, the lines were so well known to those who knew them that the film-makers felt forced at times to pay them some respect, and it is a mistake to think that in the four films preceding *Henry V* the text was entirely shot to pieces, suffer though it often did from extraordinary hiatus. In any case, audiences were being familiarised to some extent with 'talking heads' in the many filmed plays with which the era of the 'talkies' had opened.

Mary Pickford and Douglas Fairbanks, doyens of the silent cinema, started the age of sound for Shakespeare with their *The Taming of the Shrew*, still a highly viewable version of one of Shakespeare's lesser, knockabout plays. The fact that the most famous marriage in Hollywood was breaking up at the time they appeared in their only picture together added a certain spice to the horseplay in their performances. The film was well-mounted, designed by William Cameron Menzies and Laurence Irving, grandson of England's great actor-director, Henry Irving. A fly in the ointment was the notorious caption inserted by the director Sam Wood, crediting himself with "additional dialogue". Indeed, the film was made with what Laurence Irving calls "unsophisticated zeal" and was hung around with gags like any other Hollywood comedy. Constance Collier was employed as "English-speaking governess to the production". Had Shakespeare been around he would no doubt have been delighted with the vigorous treatment accorded so prentice a work. But the film had little success. Mary Pickford thought it a disaster.

But the middle 1930s saw two spectacular productions from a Hollywood notably recovering from the economic slump. Warner Brothers, looking for genius on the cheap, had absorbed much talent forced to leave Europe, and *A Midsummer Night's Dream*, with its flying ballet of fairies, its macabre dwarfs, its forest scintillating with special effects, was an impressive piece of Germanic photo-magic. It had been sponsored by Warner's in honour of Max Reinhardt, the veteran master of the German theatre, who directed it with the assistance of one of his former protégés, William Dieterle, who was already established as one of Warner's contract directors. The lines were severely cut (over half of one of Shakespeare's shortest plays disappeared) for the sake of the spectacle which Warner's expected to sell the picture, along with a roster of their contract players and other stars, including James Cagney, Ian Hunter, Dick Powell, Joe E.

Orlando in Czinner's *As You Like It* (1936).

Brown, Anita Louise, Olivia de Havilland, Victor Jory, and Mickey Rooney as Puck, a lively boy player who would surely have delighted Shakespeare. On the sound track Mendelssohn vied with Shakespeare, and the whole concept of the film derived from Reinhardt's celebrated international stage production with which he had toured both Britain and America. However, the formula for Shakespeare on the screen seemed to have been established — cut back the text, lay on the stars, build up the spectacle and play the action for all it was worth.

But it was the other two films which gave Olivier his cue for *serving*, as distinct from merely exploiting Shakespeare on the screen. George Cukor's *Romeo and Juliet* was a highly respectable, heavily capitalised MGM production of the play. MGM's insurance policy at the box-office followed the formula — stars and spectacle. The Italian background (streets, piazzas, and a wonderful garden setting for the balcony scene) was up to the highest standard of MGM's lavishness, and the stars were impeccable, led by Leslie Howard, Norma Shearer,

John Barrymore and Basil Rathbone. With such players, plenty of the text was left intact, and was indeed published in a special film edition of the play. What Howard (aged 43) and Shearer (aged 32) did with the adolescent lovers was to load the lines with experienced professional ardour rather than with poetry, treating their lovers with the maximum screen realism allowable considering the dialogue was in verse.

What Olivier specially noticed, now that, for the first time, Shakespeare's highly-charged verse was being spoken before the camera, was that the visual emphasis of the film medium often ran counter to the verbal emphasis of Shakespearian speech. The speeches normally build in speaking, starting diminuendo, working up to fortissimo. The film's basic emphasis is the close-shot, coming as climax to a series of middle, long or more distanced shots. Experienced film actors, used to scaling their performances to the camera's distance from them, kept their handling of speech diminuendo, that is, understanding when they were in close shot, with the result that climactic lines were diminished in delivery as the camera either tracked into or cut to close-shot; in any case the actors spoke the verse as if they would have preferred it to be prose. Thus film and play were at loggerheads, and the verse-speaking (weak in any case since most of the stars however experienced as players were inexperienced in Shakespeare) was in general unsatisfactory.

Olivier's first direct experience of playing Shakespeare for the screen was in *As You Like It* under the direction of Paul Czinner, a film made in Britain at the cost of around one million dollars. The production had an impressive facade — music by Sir William Walton, choreography by Ninette de Valois, and design by René Clair's distinguished art director, Lazare Meerson. The supporting cast came from the cream of the British theatre establishment — Henry Ainley, Leon Quartermaine (who as Jacques spoke the "Seven Ages" speech as if he were at Stratford-upon-Avon or the Old Vic), John Laurie and Felix Aylmer. Even Carl Mayer, Germany's most imaginative screenwriter of the silent period, now in exile in England, shared a script credit. But Czinner miscast his wife, Elizabeth Bergner, as Rosalind, a character decades later Vanessa Redgrave was to catch so well upon the stage. Elizabeth Bergner was an arch, fey, impish, coquettish, wriggling Rosalind, speaking her lines with a German accent in softly coy coo. She was a star determined to enchant.

Olivier came into the cast as Orlando with considerable experience in both theatre and film. He was still under thirty, and had recently been starring in Shakespeare in the theatre when in 1935

Cry God for Harry: *Henry V* (1944)

he had interchanged with John Gielgud the parts of Mercutio and Romeo in Gielgud's production of *Romeo and Juliet* at the New Theatre, London.

Both Gielgud and Olivier were to become in the 1930s masters of spoken Shakespeare, but with a difference in approach — Gielgud maintaining the transcendent romantic line (though with a growing strength and resilience in his melodious voice) and Olivier acquiring a certain heroic flavour of toughness, along with a "new realism" in his more "earthy" attitude to the characters, but without loss of dramatic poetry. But as Orlando he could achieve little in a production which made the Rosalind of Elizabeth Bergner its centre point. He played with quiet, male determination in the broad romantic tradition of the stage lover, and looked well on the screen, though with an interesting, darkling quality.

What mattered was what could be learnt while passing through the experience of seeing Shakespeare 'processed' in a film studio. The fake realism of the studio set, but with real sheep which only served to make it appear worse, looked and felt absurd.

Shakespeare's plays are stylised by the very nature of being conceived in terms of dramatic poetry, a stylisation offset and enhanced by his constant resort to touches of psychological naturalism and the intrusion of the everyday of his time. The virile imagination of the dramatic poetry, which takes full possession on the stage, outdoes attention to the theatre set, which at its best forms a suitable visual-atmospheric frame for the general mood of the play, and which in Shakespeare's day did not exist at all in the so-called private theatres.

In the Shakespearian films of the 1930s, the sets weighed down on the productions, and threw the whole enterprise out of gear, so when Olivier was invited in the mid-war years to direct the great 'patriotic' play of *Henry V* (ostensibly to coincide with the period of the D-Day landings in France), he accepted. He had played Henry under Tyrone Guthrie's direction at the Old Vic in 1937, and savoured the character's toughness, and he welcomed the opportunity to use colour and to counter in filming Shakespeare some of the techniques he believed to have gone wrong in the past.

His producer, without whom neither *Henry V* nor *Hamlet* would ever have been made, was Filippo de Giudice, a volatile Italian lawyer with grandiose ideas who had become manager of the British company, Two Cities Films, and who had a genius for sponsoring films of quality, including *In Which We Serve* (when he took a similar risk in giving Noël Coward his first film as director), *Brief Encounter* (which finally made David Lean's name as a director), *The Way Ahead* and *Odd Man Out*, the last two fully establishing Carol Reed as a major British director. He had a flair not only for developing talent but for cajoling financial backing; his daring in both fields frequently paid off, though the industry eventually defeated him in the 1950s. He entered a Benedictine monastery in Italy and died in 1961. But de Giudice's brilliance and generosity as an impresario was indispensable to Olivier's development both as film-maker and as pioneer in the costly business of giving Shakespeare his first fully-considered treatment on the screen. Moreover, with only one precious Technicolor camera left in wartime Britain, Olivier was permitted to make the film in colour, though this would add greatly to the time-consuming difficulties of lighting and shooting at Denham studios and on location in neutral Eire.

The film was originally budgeted at £300,000; its actual cost rose to £475,000. But de Giudice backed Olivier through thick and thin in order that the film should reach a successful conclusion. The result fully justified his confidence.

Work began on the script in 1943, Olivier working with a trusted friend, the theatre and film critic, Alan Dent. The play, though not a long one, was cut by about one-third, but scenes were also added, notably the death of Falstaff (from *Henry IV*, *Part 2*) and the spectacular battle of Agincourt shot in Eire. The film opened with an establishing sequence which showed the play being presented in an Elizabethan theatre, Shakespeare's Globe, which one saw initially in a long travelling shot like a vast aerial view of London of the 1590s. Once the performance had begun, the frame of the theatre setting was abandoned and the play and the film became one. The cuts made were not only designed to shorten what had to be said, but to erase the less 'heroic' aspects of Henry's kingly character as it was conceived to be in Shakespeare's time — his tyrannical attitude to Scotland in Act I, his ruthless handling of the plot to assassinate him by Cambridge, Scroop and Grey, his tirade at Harfleur when he threatens the city with bloodshed, rape and pillage, and his notorious order to his soldiers to kill the French prisoners-of-war. Henry is therefore 'cleaned up' to make him a hero suitable for modern times.

Olivier had then to consider the visual setting for the film, which he placed in the hands of Paul Sheriff, Carmen Dillon and Roger Furse. Having colour at their disposal, Olivier and his designers decided to give the film a late medieval, early Renaissance heraldic appearance. They turned to the Limbourg illustrations for the Duc de Berry's "Calendar of the Book of Hours" and the illustrations to Froissart's "Chronicles". Olivier was determined at all costs to avoid realism in the palace and castle settings, even to the point of adopting the foreshortened perspective and virtually non-furnished decor of the medieval backgrounds in which the leading characters were drawn to a scale commensurate with their social status. Robert Krasker's camerawork matched these medieval splendours, with its pateant-like decoration. At times in the film this leads to visual curiosities — for example, Henry's wooing of Katharine is played very naturalistically as the dialogue warrants, but is nevertheless set in decor with a purely medieval perspective which is really only acceptable in association with stylised, static human figures.

Only the theatre setting at the beginning and end of the film, and a few shots of London alleyways, had a more realistic appearance, except, naturally enough, the location shots for Agincourt in the fields of Lord Powerscourt's estate at Enniskerry, near Dublin. The Agincourt sequence (influenced to some extent by the charge of the Teutonic knights in Eisenstein's film, *Alexander Nevsky*) was begun in June 1943. The unit was plagued by bad

With the Dean of Westminster at the 1971 restoration of the tomb of Henry V.

weather and it became a costly enterprise; 180 horsemen and 500 footmen from the Irish Home Guard fought the battle on waterlogged ground, and for the famous tracking-shot of the charge, a rail-track had to be laid for about a mile along a farm-road to give the travelling camera smooth passage. The rest of the film was shot at Denham, finishing in early January 1944, and the film was completed in July. D-Day was on 6 June.

The film was a remarkable achievement for a first venture by a young actor-director. It was dominated by Olivier's own presence — he plays Henry with a vigorous, naturalistic humour which suits exactly the varied nature of Shakespeare's writing, ranging from the heroic oratory of Henry's address to the army before Agincourt to the contemplative poetry of his thoughts as he moves through his camp, silent and unrecognised, the night before battle, and the quiet, gentle humour of the prose scenes of the wooing of Katharine. Olivier was able to try out the reverse principle in the film technique he had felt necessary after seeing *Romeo and Juliet*. Contrary to the standard practice of film technique, he took the camera *away* from Henry for the climactic utterance when the voice must be loud and resonant, the gesture broad, the expression strong and emphatic as on the stage — for which, after all, the speech had been written.

The camera begins by tracking beside Henry as he walks along the ranks of his men, talking at natural pitch, then gradually pulls back to take in the whole scene as he leaps on to a cart and allows his voice

to build towards the climax of the speech. This over, he leaps straight from the cart onto horseback, and words give way to action and movement, "God be with you all". The needs of both Shakespeare and the film are exactly satisfied, and when Olivier wheels into close shot on his horse, he drops his voice into self-address, a moment of intimacy, "And how thou pleasest, God, dispose the day".

In the charge of the French knights initiating the battle of Agincourt — which one must emphasise is not in the play at all, but provides its own visually dramatic climax within the broad structure of the play — William Walton's music supplies the heroic theme as horsemen and foot-soldiers are joined in battle, locked in a vast human tangle viewed from above in a composition which recalls Uccello's "Rout of San Romano". The whirr of the mass-flight of arrows comes as a climax built into the crescendo of the music, and the cries and clangour of armour and swordplay take over. Walton's rousing music for the film — now a pastiche in the Elizabethan mode, now direct action-music, now a gentle, suggestive under-pinning of the spoken word (as in the beautiful Chorus speech describing the preparations in camp the night before Agincourt) — acts cohesively to bind the film together in mood and atmosphere.

The other casting, too, was in general, excellent, including Leslie Banks (Chorus), Max Adrian (Dauphin), Renée Asherson (Katherine) and Robert Newton (Pistol).

31

"Whether 'tis nobler in the mind . . ."

Many scenes are memorable both as film and as Shakespeare — Mistress Quickly's (Freda Jackson's) lamentation over the body of Falstaff (George Robey), the moving speech of the common soldier about the King spoken in a West-country accent and, above all, in the quiet lines spoken so magnificently by Olivier on the sound track as the King wanders round the camp at night to see that all is well with his men and soliloquises on the position and responsibilities of a medieval monarch. Here the camera became the King, seeing what he saw, the men asleep, the camp and its armour poised at rest.

The offer to make *Hamlet* followed hard upon the success of *Henry V* — success, that is, of esteem because it took some years before the print cost of *Henry V* was recovered and the picture moved gradually from loss to profit. Against his real wish he was forced to play Hamlet as well as direct the film — "I feel that my style of acting is more suited to stronger character roles . . . rather than to the lyrical, poetical role of Hamlet", he wrote. He dyed his hair blonde perhaps as much to dis-identify himself from the part as to give his appearance a Scandinavian touch.

As a film director, however, he welcomed the challenge that a film of Shakespeare's most complex play represented.

The film was to be shot in black-and-white, using deep-focus photography to exploit distant vistas and perspectives, allowing actors to be clearly registered up to 150 feet from the camera. Desmond Dickinson took over the camera direction and Helga Cranston the editing, but otherwise the key creative team from *Henry V* remained the same, design in the hands of Carmen Dillon and Roger Furse, the music (directed again by Muir Mathieson) composed by William Walton. The leading players were Basil Sydney (Claudius), Eileen Herlie (Gertrude), Jean Simmons (Ophelia), Felix Aylmer (Polonius), Terence Morgan (Laertes) and Stanley Holloway (the Gravedigger). Jean Simmons was still young and inexperienced; Eileen Herlie, very young in appearance, brought a faint suggestion of a more than natural love between mother and son. There is jealousy in Hamlet's hatred of Claudius.

In my view, *Hamlet* is by far the most interesting of Olivier's three pioneer, and very different, attempts to film Shakespeare. This is obviously due in part to the enormous demands it makes on the imagination and comprehension of the audience compared with the far less demanding *Henry V* and *Richard III*, in which the difficulties are more on the level of maintaining clarity in the progress of the plot and action than comprehension of character. In handling the text of *Hamlet*, Olivier favoured wholesale cutting, however controversial, rather than a finicky trimming of the text. So we lose not only two of the major soliloquies ("O what a rogue and peasant slave am I" and "How all occasions do inform against me"), but also three major characters — Rosencrantz and Guildenstern, and Fortinbras — and several memorable scenes, such as the scene in which the Ghost intervenes from below ground with the repetition of the word "Swear" and the First Player's set-speech about Priam.

In addition, some 25 words in the text were changed to clarify meaning for the untutored audience ("hinders" for "lets", for example). These cuts, changes and other alterations were to lead to controversy in the correspondence columns of *The Times* and in BBC debate when the film was shown. Olivier's interpretation skirts the Renaissance man of action latent in Hamlet's nature and stresses the romantic, contemplative, melancholy, dilatory aspect of the Prince. The soliloquies become in film terms spoken thought, often without lip movement, but sometimes with lip movement introduced suddenly to mark some special, obsessive thought — "perchance to dream". The handling of the Ghost is subtle — its presence perceived at first only through the reaction of Hamlet and his companions on the darkened battlements, later seen in close-up like a bearded skull shadowed deep in the cavities of its helmet. The Ghost's speech was recorded by Olivier himself, but played back slightly under speed to achieve an unearthly quality. Hamlet's mounting heartbeats (an impressionistic effect borrowed from Jean-Louis Barrault's stage production) convey the horror of the experience. When the Ghost departs, Hamlet collapses, a prone figure lying in the narrow circle of the tower. All these effects reinforce the play, but in terms which belong naturally to film. Close-up is frequently used with marked effect, not only in the soliloquies but at such intense moments as Hamlet's contemplation of Yorick's skull.

The dramatic bravura Olivier loves is seen when action is at last realised. The duel at the end of the film is stretched to an action lasting ten minutes, a brilliantly edited sequence which took many days to shoot. The final climax of revenge is marked by Hamlet's flying leap from a balcony down onto Claudius, his sword driven into the King's body by the sheer force of the fall — the last shot to be made for the film in case Olivier sustained injury. The funeral march with which the film closes, when Hamlet's body is borne in state to the tower, is one of Walton's finest compositions for Olivier's Shakespearian films. On occasion, as in *Henry V*, he uses period pastiche, notably for the players' mime before the King, but in his principal themes develops an imperial music which gives grandeur to to a film which, for all its occasional lapses and longueurs, deserved to the full the acclaim it received — four Oscars (including that for the best film of the year and for best actor) and the Grand Prix at the 1948 Venice Film Festival.

It was not until the mid-1950s that Olivier was given an opportunity to make a third Shakespearian film. The offer came eventually through the producer, Alexander Korda, and the play chosen (not altogether to Olivier's liking) was *Richard III*, partly because of Olivier's remarkable characterisation of Richard, Duke of Gloucester, at the Old Vic in 1944 and partly because, with a logic that remains obscure, it was thought that the play with its coronation scenes fitted the times, with the coronation of Queen Elizabeth in 1953. At first Olivier hoped that Carol Reed might share the burden by directing the film, but finally he was forced, yet again, both to direct and play the leading character. He kept the same basic team with him — Roger Furse and Carmen Dillon as designers, Helga Cranston as editor, Alan Dent as text editor, and William Walton as composer. The film was to be shot in colour using the new VistaVision system which offered a semi-widescreen image; the director of photography was Otto Heller. The actor, Anthony Bushell, who had acted as Olivier's assistant director on *Hamlet*, worked with him also on *Richard III*.

Talking to me about his approach to this film, Olivier said, "The same basic problems remain, of reducing the length, elucidating the plot, unravelling irrelevancies, and relating the result to the type of audience." Shakespeare's play, although an early one, has always been popular because it has offered actors through all the generations since Shakespeare's own time a great bravura character to play, a villain of the worst kind but one enlivened and humanised by possessing a sardonic sense of humour and a desire to share his villainy with his audience. The combination is irresistible, and Olivier's performance for the Old Vic, allying old-style melodrama with a modern sense of the character's paranoiac qualities, excited new speculations about Shakespeare's dimension as a character-builder. Richard was his first major venture in the field of providing great actors with a part worthy of their skill.

The "delta" (as Olivier termed it) of the plot at the beginning was opened up to allow the action to point forward to the free flow of story which only begins about one-third through the play. The age of television had arrived, and since the mass-audience was now well used to being addressed directly from the screen (and so 'involved' in the illusion by being spoken to), Olivier decided to let Richard act as 'anchor-man' to the film, at least at the beginning. So he talks to the audience, letting them into his grand conspiracy to seize the throne by underhand and violent means.

After the coronation of Edward IV (a scene taken from *King Henry VI, Part 3)* with which the film opens, Richard creeps around the palace like a conspirator making it plain to the audience who everyone is and why it is necessary to remove now this person, now that, in order to achieve the crown for himself. Words are constantly clarified by images, the palace conspiracy made plain. The theme of the film is betrayal, and no one in the audience was unaware in the 1950s of the parallel between Richard III and Hitler in the seizure of power by treachery, the false face presented to friend and foe alike. The most remarkable sequence in the film is the celebrated six-minute take covering Richard's speech beginning, "Now is the winter of our discontent . . .", the lines augmented by other of his thoughts taken from later in the play and from *Henry VI, Part 3*. This is played in an L-shaped throne room, with Olivier carrying out his familiar principle of scaling the volume of the speech to his distance from the camera; he moves up to it to share more intimate thought and away from it for mom-

"No beast so fierce but knows some touch of pity".
Richard III (1955).

ents of paranoiac outburst; he even takes it for a walk from one wing of the hall to the other, sharing his confidences with a knowing leer. There can be no doubt what is in Richard's mind, but to make sure, he opens window-shutters and doors to point out to whom he is referring. He hypnotises the Lady Anne (Claire Bloom) into consenting to be his wife, though she knows he murdered her previous husband.

The scene, so difficult to accept in other than abnormal psychological terms, is made absolutely

34

credible, all the more because it is split by a time-lapse into two parts to allow her to fall the more completely under his noxious spell. Thus everything is done to make the play not only clear but acceptable in modern, naturalistic terms. Richard laughs with the audience at his success with this innocent victim — "Was ever woman in this humour woo'd?" Violence and humour go hand in hand in this historical melodrama — Clarence (another innocent) is murdered in the Tower, and his body thrust splashing into a vast butt of wine. Buckingham (an ally none the less betrayed, as Hitler betrayed Roehm) is threatened macabrely when Richard suddenly slides down a bellrope and, before Buckingham can recover, asserts his baneful authority over the man who, more than any other, has helped him to power. Richard leans from the throne he has for so long coveted like some greedy snake craning forward to swallow his prey whole.

In the realisation of this film, Olivier had his most distinguished cast yet. In addition to Claire Bloom, it included Cedric Hardwicke (Edward IV), John Gielgud (Clarence), Ralph Richardson (Buckingham), Stanley Baker (Richmond). Yet again, the decor was experimental, the topography of medieval London being entirely abandoned so that the characters could move directly between the principal centres of action, Westminster, the Palace, and the Tower. The battle of Bosworth was reconstructed in Spain (however improbable the landscape) to ensure fine weather in shooting against time; Olivier did not intend to suffer as he had done ten years before in Ireland. The film was brought in, most efficiently, at a cost well under that of either *Henry V* or *Hamlet*.

After *Richard III*, Olivier strove for nearly a year to set up a film of *Macbeth*, which would have been successor to Glen Byam Shaw's stage production of the play at Stratford-upon-Avon in 1955, with Vivien Leigh as Lady Macbeth and himself as Macbeth. But he failed to obtain the necessary £400,000 backing. He was, however, to appear in two further screen adaptations from Shakespeare, *Othello* (1965), directed by Stuart Burge and based directly upon John Dexter's celebrated production for the National Theatre, and *The Merchant of Venice* (1973), directed by Jonathan Miller and based on his production for the National Theatre in 1970.

Both of these were screen records of essentially theatrical versions of the plays, the first presenting one of the most remarkable feats of acting in Olivier's entire career and the second an interesting, semi-modernised transposition of the action of the play from the Elizabethan period to the late 19th century. Both, though drawing little on film technique as such, are most valuable records from the theatre, more especially the first. Both were made in colour.

Nothing in Olivier's career brought him quite the same level of public response as his Negro *Othello*, which became the subject of a book by Kenneth Tynan ("*Othello, The National Theatre Production*", 1966), special photo-coverages in *Life*, and the like. On the other hand, since the muted, near-naturalistic performances by other principal members of the cast, notably Frank Finlay (Iago — considered as underplayed upon the stage), Maggie Smith (Desdemona), and Robert Lang (Roderigo) are scaled to the proximity of the camera, the titanic force of Olivier's interpretation, wholly geared to the distancing of the theatre, appears on big screen (as distinct from television) over-enlarged. It is a pity that both direction, camera coverage and performance were not more firmly and designedly matched to give this great and controversial interpretation (for which Olivier specially developed his voice to encompass a deeper octave) its maximum effect on the big screen. It was, after all, being transposed into a film intended for distribution to audiences who did not see the production in the theatre, and would therefore only comprehend it as it was transferred to the screen.

Olivier's Shylock, cityman Jew in a TV version of *The Merchant of Venice*, clothed in the morning coats and shiny top hats of the Forsyte period, was a subtly conceived characterisation, full of sardonic observation and humour, but capable of paroxysms of rage. He conceived his Jew as a racially sensitive rich man, a would-be sophisticated gentleman, at once ingratiating and sinister in the company of Gentiles. He speaks with elaborate care, striving to catch the affected speech characteristic of the racy Victorian gentleman, dropping his final "gs" with studied care and mincing his "ows". But the iron will is concealed beneath the fop's tongue. Shylock becomes the centre of gravity of the play, his loathing of the Gentiles with whom he is forced to do business and who mock him and spurn his race building to a climax when one of them steals his daughter. His defeat in the court of law, though necessary to stay the savagery of his revenge, brings honour to nobody, while Jessica's future happiness with Lorenzo, a Jewess isolated among the Belmont set of late Victorian playboys ruled by their rich hostess Portia (Joan Plowright), is obviously in serious doubt.

The racialism in the play is heavily underlined. Olivier's characterisation of Shylock belongs to the wonderful gallery of eccentrics he had created on the stage from Shallow to Teazle, and from Tattle to Archie Rice.

With Marilyn Monroe in *The Prince and the Showgirl* (1958).

OLIVIER: THE POSTWAR YEARS

BY SHERIDAN MORLEY

Setting aside his prewar (see Dilys Powell), Shakespearian (see Roger Manvell) and guest-starring (see Tom Hutchinson) work in the cinema, Olivier has thus far (1977) made major appearances in fifteen postwar films, two of which (*The Prince and The Showgirl*, 1957, and *The Three Sisters*, 1970) he also directed. Of those fifteen, five were based in one way or another on work he had already done for the stage; a further four were Hollywood period pieces and one was *The Beggar's Opera* (1953) while another (*The Power and The Glory*, 1961) is only a film in European terms since it was made initially for American television. Thus of that first fifteen we are now left with only four original modern-dress screenplays in which Olivier has played sizeable roles (Peter Glenville's *Term of Trial*, 1962, Otto Preminger's *Bunny Lake Is Missing*, 1965, Joseph Mankiewicz's *Sleuth*, 1973, and John Schlesinger's *Marathon Man*, 1976) a statistic which may perhaps go some way toward explaining why Olivier has remained for more than thirty years now the head of his profession in the theatre but has never, in some curious way, been considered our leading film star.

When Olivier went out to Hollywood in 1951 to start work on *Carrie* he had done nothing on the screen since the middle of the war except Shakespeare and a fleeting moment in *The Magic Box*. He went to do *Carrie* (after Cary Grant had refused it) primarily because it was for William Wyler who had given him his first great Hollywood success in *Wuthering Heights* twelve years previously and who had taught him, Olivier now admits, most of what he knows about film acting. Indeed it had been Olivier's forlorn hope that Wyler would direct him in the Shakespeare films. He also went back to Hollywood at this time because his then wife, Vivien Leigh, was filming *A Streetcar Named Desire* in California and at that period Olivier seldom liked to let the temperamental Miss Leigh get too far out of his sight.

Based on Theodore Dreiser's novel (*Sister Carrie*,

the *Sister* being dropped by Wyler lest audiences should think it was a nun's story), and co-starring Jennifer Jones, it was a somewhat heavy-handed 'Star is Born' account of a man's inadvertent destruction by the woman he loves, and as a film it fell with a terrible thud at the box-office. Critics who went to it looking for an actor found Olivier as impressive as ever; those who went looking for a film star found him 'stagey' — a word that was to haunt Olivier in modern-dress films thereafter, though Wyler himself reckoned that "Larry's 'Hurstwood' is the truest and best portrayal of an American by an Englishman I have ever seen".

Olivier's next screen appearance was in the first film of a 27-year-old Peter Brook: *The Beggar's Opera* (1953). It, too, did less than triumphant business at the box-office: Brook, who had reputedly first considered Richard Burton for the rôle, was to note later that it had taken nine more years before he was offered another film: "When you flop to the tune of a quarter of a million pounds, you have to do penance".

With Danny Kaye (left) and Sid Field (right) at the Café de Paris, 1949.

"Triplets": Danny Kaye, Vivien Leigh, Laurence Olivier — London Palladium, 1954.

With Marilyn on the *Prince and the Showgirl* set, August 1956.

There seem to have been basic disagreements between Brook and Olivier on aspects of the character of Macheath, but the reviews were generally more favourable for the actor than the director. The former also did his own singing, which is more than could be said for some others in the cast.

Five years and *Richard III* separated *The Beggar's Opera* from *The Prince and The Showgirl* (1957), the film Olivier made of Terence Rattigan's regal drawing-room comedy *The Sleeping Prince*. Written originally for Sir Laurence and Vivien Leigh to do on the West End stage as a *divertissement* during Coronation year, it had always been a thin script though it was to prove surprisingly durable — after its film adaptation it reappeared five years later as a Broadway musical (with songs by Noël Coward) entitled *The Girl Who Came To Supper*.

For the screen, Olivier's co-star was Marilyn Monroe whom he had agreed also to direct, a double which proved more than a little fraught as Miss Monroe was not then at her easiest. The result was an elegant, artificial period piece through which Olivier and Monroe moved on two separate planets, seldom in their styles even appearing to inhabit the same movie, yet remaining consistently watchable and true to their own respective notions of what the film was about.

The Devil's Disciple, which Olivier made in the following year for Guy Hamilton (who was to direct him again a decade later in *The Battle of Britain*) was filmed while he was still trying to raise the money for his long-projected but ultimately abortive film of *Macbeth*: fund-raising which involved not only having to make other movies in the meantime, but also having to quiet the lingering American fear

that he was less than magic at the box-office. In the event, and looking at the film with the wisdom of hindsight, it would seem that wherever else Olivier's heart may have been it was not in the making of *The Devil's Disciple*.

Nevertheless, playing General Burgoyne (one of the few characters allowed to remain more or less as Shaw wrote him) Olivier effortlessly stole the picture from Burt Lancaster as Anderson and Kirk Douglas as Dudgeon — a theft which would have been still more intriguing had it been a film worth stealing.

Two years later, in 1960, Olivier filmed for Tony Richardson the performance which surely represents him at his absolute non-Shakespearian best. The part of Archie Rice, the rundown pier comic who is *The Entertainer*, was one he had first created in John Osborne's play at the Royal Court theatre in 1957. At that time, the notion of England's leading classical actor allying himself with the 'angry young men' at the Court caused considerable Press comment. But what Olivier had recognised in *The Entertainer* was not simply the chance to get away (in his non-classical work) from an already moribund West End, but also one of the great theatrical parts of all time. Archie Rice ("You see this face — it can split open with warmth and humanity. It can sing, and tell the worst, unfunniest stories in the world to a great mob of dead, drab erks and it doesn't matter, it doesn't matter. It doesn't matter because — look at my eyes. I'm dead behind these eyes. I'm dead, just like the whole inert, shoddy lot out there") is a giant among Olivier rôles and, although the film experienced a certain amount of trouble in opening up the original and more claustrophobic stage play, it was ludicrously under-rated

With Vivien Leigh, Marilyn Monroe and her husband Arthur Miller at London's Comedy Theatre

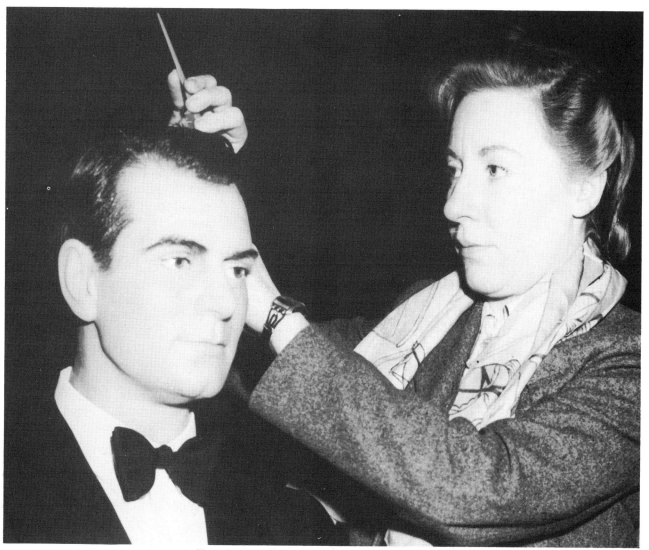

The waxwork Olivier: Madame Tussaud's, 1950.

With Kirk Douglas, Janette Scott and Burt Lancaster filming *The Devil's Disciple* (1958).

by many critics and remains the first place I should take a newcomer who was searching for the measure of Olivier's greatness on camera.

In 1960 Olivier made his first epic — *Spartacus*, written by Dalton Trumbo from Howard Fast's bestseller and directed by Stanley Kubrick. Widely regarded by critics on both sides of the Atlantic as the most intelligent of the road-show blockbusters made in those golden times (the film took a year and twelve million dollars to produce) *Spartacus* also offered its customers Kirk Douglas, Tony Curtis, Jean Simmons, Charles Laughton and Peter Ustinov who won that year's supporting-actor Oscar. But Olivier's performance as Crassus remains the most intriguing, albeit somewhat hard to judge since a crucial scene in which he attempted to seduce Tony Curtis was heavily cut, presumably on the grounds that American audiences were not yet ready for glimpses of Roman homosexuality.

In 1962 Olivier was back in modern dress for *Term of Trial*, a sort of latterday *Carrie* most notable now for having introduced both Sarah Miles and Terence Stamp to the screen. The plot, about the destructive effects of teenagers on adult relationships, also featured Simone Signoret whose scenes with Olivier were the highlight of an otherwise rather shadowy venture.

In 1965, staying in modern dress, Olivier played the Scotland Yard police inspector for Otto Preminger in *Bunny Lake Is Missing*, a thoroughly competent if rather muted thriller dignified by its minor-part casting (Noël Coward, Anna Massey, Martita Hunt) and by a literate script from John and Penelope Mortimer. By now, though, Olivier was giving virtually all his time to the administration of the National Theatre, and his appearance in the following years as the Mahdi in *Khartoum*, though vocally and physically unforgettable, was in fact little more than a wide-screen exaggeration of his then current National *Othello*.

The next two films he made, outside of cameos, were both on behalf of the National Theatre, and both were photographic records of distinguished stage productions: *The Dance of Death* in 1969 and *The Three Sisters* (which he also directed) in 1970. Both films hovered, in Dilys Powell's phrase, "on the very margin of cinema" and both clearly had an American television aim as well.

Olivier's real return to the cinema did not then come until 1972, in which year his impending resignation from the administration of the National was announced. The film he chose to come back with was *Sleuth*, Tony Shaffer's complex two-handed thriller in which Olivier co-starred with Michael

Caine for the veteran American director Joseph L. Mankiewicz. Typically, Olivier had selected for his return not a vehicle but a challenge: in its contorted intensity and in its lengthy speeches, the part of Andrew Wyke must be among the longest and most demanding in the modern cinema.

Though it failed to win him the Oscar he so clearly deserved for it, *Sleuth* once again established Olivier as a screen force to be reckoned with; "acting with him" said Michael Caine, "was rather like acting with God".

The critic of *Newsweek* was in no doubt that *Sleuth* was "a kind of miracle" and that Olivier was "spellbinding" as Wyke. But three full years were to elapse before he was able to give another real film performance: three years in which he'd made occasional guest appearances on stage and screen but throughout which he had had to battle with a crippling and wasting disease of the muscles. Coming as this did at the end of a decade in which Olivier had also had to contend with both cancer and thrombosis, it might have been expected that there would never again be a major performance from him.

The stage, as he himself said, was now "too exhausting" for him to contemplate the long-promised *King Lear*, and instead he announced he'd be searching for some "dazzling little cameos" in the cinema and on television to see him painlessly through his old age.

That was what he said in a number of Press interviews during 1974: those accustomed, however, to the often startling difference between what Olivier says he is going to do and what he then does were not altogether surprised to find him less than a year later taking on the sizeable co-starring role opposite Dustin Hoffman in John Schlesinger's *Marathon Man*, though many were relieved and delighted to discover that the professional and private battles he had had to fight throughout the late 60s and early 70s (at the National Theatre and at a succession of hospitals) had left his screen strength not only unimpaired but in some intriguing way even apparently heightened.

In *Marathon Man*, Olivier plays a prominent Nazi who has been in hiding since the fall of the Third Reich but who now seeks, in New York a quarter of a century later, to retrieve an illegal fortune that he has stashed away. Early sneak-preview audiences in California were reportedly amazed by the sustained level of the violence, notably in Olivier's gruesome death scene, but in England *The Times* noted that "Olivier is always at his best in performances that call for him to be seedy or nasty or both" and this particular one won him a Variety Club award for the actor of the year. It was not his first: nor, I suspect, will it necessarily be his last.

With Kenneth More at Evelyn Laye's 70th birthday, 1970.

In drag for the "Night of 100 Stars", London Palladium, 1960.

With Anna Neagle and their 1949 *Picturegoer* Awards.

With the editor of Pears' Cyclopedia, receiving a *Richard III* trophy.

With Gina Lollobrigida, receiving the 1962 "Olympus" award for his services to the international theatre.

Receiving the Sonning Prize from the University of Copenhagen, 1950.

Greeting H.R.H. Princess Anne at the Cameo-Poly cinema for the Royal Charity première of Olivier's production of *Three Sisters*

43

On the beat as the stolid Holborn policeman in *The Magic Box*

OLIVIER: THE GUEST STAR
BY TOM HUTCHINSON

Although the makers of films often seem to think that they are adding to the lustre of their product by including, within the framework of their movies, a few minutes of guest-appearance by some actor whose presence is deemed necessary in terms of marquee billing and front-of-house advertising, too often a groan of apprehension goes up from the critic who sits knowing —with a prescience that is explicable by past boredom — what to expect.

For what such an appearance means in general is a halt in the story, a stutter in the narrative, while the audience adjusts the sights of its comprehension to an inclusion which is, tiresomely, an intrusion. So-called 'cameo-roles' usually add nothing to the story beyond the addition of a promotable name and they often detract because, however hard one tries, the temptation is always there to stop suspending disbelief and say, "Oh, look, it's old so-and-so." The celebrity-actor defeats the object of the story-telling exercise in such a context.

It is my belief that this has never happened with any of Laurence Olivier's guest-appearances in films; his insertion into a plot does not stick out like a sore thumb. Rather, to shift the medical analogy, it is as well-polished into place, and as hard to recognise from the rest of the film's mood or characterisation, as a discreetly-crafted filling in a tooth. He has said, "My earliest feelings about acting were suffused with an intense wish to fascinate the public in the art of acting." It is part of his selfless genius that he has been able to sublimate the Olivier persona, as it were, so that we were most distinctly aware of his guest-rôle only afterwards — not during.

Perhaps the most submerged of all his guest-appearances was that of the astonished policeman in *The Magic Box* (1951), which detailed the wistful aspirations of the British inventor, William Friese-Greene, to have public recognition of the fact that he had created the cinematograph. Robert Donat played the unrewarded inventor, in what was to be a Festival of Britain flop. In the scene in which he sees the first flickers of motion cast on to a white sheet he hurries out into the night to capture a witness of the event.

It is a witness of obvious respectability, a British bobby of the time with bull's-eye lantern and eyes looking par-boiled with astonishment. This is Olivier at work, investing the man with personality in a few lines and a few minutes, as Donat drags him protesting into the room. The policeman is convinced he is dealing with a drunk or a madman and then the pictures of people in a park shimmer into imitated life. It is on Olivier's face that we then dwell: an iron mask of fortitude across which one can just discern the rust of panic trying to break through. It is a scene that lasts a brief time, but it lingers longer in the memory.

In 1969 he made three guest-appearances in films of some distinction. "You have to choose these bit-parts" —he used the term with no sense of disparagment — "with some care, because people are going to react to the way you act; you have to be careful." The least distinguished was, possibly, Delbert Mann's version of Charles Dickens's *David Copperfield*, with Olivier as the appalling schoolmaster, Mr. Creakle. Originally made for American television, it was then released in Europe as a feature film. His portrayal was a delight because he was working with an old friend, Richard Attenborough, who was that other repellent master, Mr. Tungay. Several critics commented on their superb double-act. It was, in truth, a kind of dramatic pas-de-deux on a tightrope that crossed the chasm of caricature, into which both could have pitched headlong if they had not been so professionally adept; and so at one with each other's dramatic emphases.

Olivier's guest-visits have often been concerned with assuming the guise of real-life characters, to whom he may bear no physical resemblance in the flesh but with whom he superbly equates in the spirit. In that same year (1969) he did two such performances: as Field-Marshal Sir John French in *Oh! What A Lovely War* and as Air Chief Marshal Sir Hugh Dowding in *Battle Of Britain*.

The first was Richard Attenborough's debut as a director, translating — albeit with some purple passages that tended to suffocate the satirical spirit of the original — the musical play about the horrors

Mr Creakle in *David Copperfield* (1969).

of the First World War which had been performed by Joan Littlewood's Theatre Workshop. As French, Olivier was able to suggest the kind of upper-class mentality that was ignorant of what was happening, unknowing of the many young men being led to disaster and destruction.

Dowding — whom many experts believe tactically helped the British to win the aerial battle-in-the-air in the early days of the Second World War — was a complete character turnabout. For Dowding was a man intelligent enough to know that he had to send his young lions to their deaths and sensitive enough to feel the bereavement that such a decision would bring.

It was an appearance which allowed Olivier more time than usual to work out the way the personality should be put across — five days of filming for him — and one to which I shall return later, because of my own personal involvement with the film and the way, from the sidelines, I saw him build up the role.

Although made in 1968, *The Shoes Of The Fisherman*, in which Olivier appeared as the Russian Premier, only appeared in Britain in 1972. To keep something on the shelf as long as that implies a certain lack of freshness in the first place: the resultant odour on screening was adjudged "worthy, but a bit off."

Adapted by Morris West from his own best-seller, the story concerned a Russian priest who, after years of imprisonment in Siberia, is allowed to come in out of that particular cold and, after due process of protocol, becomes Pope. He resumes a dialogue with the Russian Premier, Kamenev, who at one time had been his interrogator, and aids him to feed the starving millions of Asia.

As a piece of political wish-fulfillment one's heart went out to it, but Anthony Quinn seemed very miscast as the Pope and it was only in Olivier that one really believed: a Man of the Party who gradually realises that he has to become a Man of the People. It would have been interesting to have seen what would have been made of the film if the rôles of Pontiff and Premier had been reversed; something might have been salvaged.

It is of the nature of things that guest-stars usually appear in epics, because it is thought that their timed inclusion — like those anti-flu tablets that take effect over a period of hours — will accelerate the story's impetus, which may well be flagging, however well-intentioned the motives. Well-intended indeed, was *Nicholas and Alexandra* (1971), Sam Spiegel's massive monument to the last days of the Romanov family and the first days of the Russian Revolution But between the milestones of those two occurrences a lot of human interest was ground out, apart from — need I say it again? — from the acting of Olivier, this time as Count Witte.

Here is a portrait of a man who has tried to plead with his sovereign to understand the plight of their country's people and to realise what might happen; a man doomed to failure in that attempted persuasion; a man forced by his nature to carry on persuading. As a study in diplomatic nobility I consider this small cameo to contain more understanding and insight than many flashier brooches. It is a picture not only of a nobleman, but of a worker in the corridors of power; knowledgeable in the ways of the world and weary of that knowledge... and of the world.

Weariness was something, presumably, that never touched the later life of the Duke of Wellington, at least not as revealed by an enthusiastic Olivier in *Lady Caroline Lamb* (1972), another acting confrontation with historical reality, but a character far enough away in time for Olivier to have room for dramatic manouevre, to take — shall we say? —

As French, with Michael Redgrave as Wilson in Attenborough's *Oh! What A Lovely War* (1969).

little liberties of interpretation.

The film concerned itself, via Robert Bolt's direction and screenplay for his then wife, Sarah Miles, with Lady Caroline whose romantic wilfulness was supposed to have irritated Byron (one can see why) and nearly confounded Wellington.

Lady Caroline importunes the latter who, while retaining the dignity of his own legend, is only too happy to be importuned. After the small affair the delight is in witnessing the way Wellington tries to discard "the dear lady," almost as though she were that boot to which he was to give his name. What emerged from this portrayal was the rounding out of a personality that seemed at once true and real, yet very much of a time that was different to ours.

One of Olivier's strengths has always been his ability to sink himself into the period, to suggest a man of that time which is his circumstance. As Sir John French there was something about the atmosphere of the man which suggested that the ground he was treading was First World War soil. As was the feeling

As the Russian Premier in *Shoes of the Fisherman* (1968).

47

with his projection as Air Chief Marshal Sir Hugh Dowding and the time of the *Battle Of Britain*.

On this film, which was being produced by Harry Saltzman and S. Benjamin Fisz, I was able to watch Olivier at work, because I was writing a book on the subject of the battle. Most of his scenes were set in R.A.F. Headquarters, which were reconstructed at Pinewood Studios. But there was an early scene, I remember, which was shot in a deserted Whitehall office early on a Sunday morning.

It was a crucial scene. It comes immediately after the Battle of Dunkirk and concerns a letter that Dowding wrote to Winston Churchill, requesting that no more fighter aircraft be sent to France, even though this meant that Churchill would have to go back on his word. This letter was read voice-over by Olivier, as he walked the whole length of the corridor, got into a creaky old lift and was clattered upstairs to see some important wartime decision-maker.

A simple enough scene, but for Olivier it had to be right. He said that he didn't want to have to rely on later editing to reconcile the time taken to walk the corridor with the time taken to read the letter. He wanted it all to coincide in one uninterrupted shot; director Guy Hamilton was happy to oblige. It took eight attempts to get it right.

The trouble with *Battle Of Britain* is that there were so many stars in it that the roll of their names — and one's recognition of them in the movie — assumed a monotonous regularity with no real dramatic point. Only Olivier managed to raise the periscope of his talent from the character in which he was submerged, to make us realise what Dowding meant as a man.

More in keeping was the less recognisable personality of Dr. Spaander in the (again star-embellished) *A Bridge Too Far*, Richard Attenborough's epic reconstruction of the Arnhem raid, with Olivier playing the leading civilian doctor in the area: a physician in his sixties but still of a remarkable energy and compassion.

As opposed to this, there was the small, but effective, study in *The Seven-Per-Cent Solution*, in which he played that arch-villain Professor Moriarty in the adaptation of Nicholas H. Meyer's pastiche of Sherlock Holmes — with Nicol Williamson as a Holmes obsessed and deranged by his hatred of a Moriarty who, despite all Conan Doyle's evidence to the contrary, here emerges as a sly, seedy, rather pathetic figure, not at all villainous and in down-right need of repair.

That characterisation, of course, gave him much scope for dramatic fun and games. Within the role of Dowding in *Battle Of Britain* he had to conform to an accepted idea of a man already alive, and work within the knowledge that the man was already a character in his own right.

I remember asking him if he had studied Dowding at all, met him, read newspaper cuttings. "No, I didn't. What I did do was read the script and look up the history books and try to understand what kind of man this would be who would go against Churchill in this kind of way and would help save a country; a man who later became a spiritualist and, I suppose, what some people would call a crank. And so, you know, I accumulated bit by bit — as a kind of instinct — that he was a kind of visionary. The kind, I think, that the Royal Air Force, of all the services, seems to attract..."

In the way that Olivier could build character without the straw of substance, I recall one scene in which Dowding is approached by two of his commanders who are arguing the respective merits of their tactics. Because of possible repercussions at the time of filming, Dowding's response took neither one side nor another. As Olivier said, "Really these words are not bloody answering the problem at all." Yet such is the power of his persuading, the intensity of his answer, that I defy any audience to realise that *nothing* has really been said in those words at all.

When the retired Dowding was brought to the studios to meet Olivier, the man who was impersonating him, the former R.A.F. leader was badly paralysed, but still articulate and proud to have his wheelchair pushed by so many of the fighter aces who were technical experts on the movie.

Olivier and he shook hands. "I apologise for not looking like you," said the much thicker-set actor, "but I am trying to *be* like you." "A thankless task, but *I* thank you," replied Dowding.

When he saw the rushes he said he thought that Olivier had succeeded; "you even forget how handsome he is."

For Olivier it was "the best compliment of all. The trouble with this bit-part is that the man I'm imitating is alive and here to criticise me if he wants to. Usually, I've played it clever and gone in for dead heroes for my guest bits. Mind you, it is true; I've always tried to *be* them. After all physique isn't what a person's all about, is it?"

Which is why Laurence Olivier is the guest you don't mind welcoming in films. He is there because it seems right that he should be there, not because he is a box-office name, the neon of whose performance will help illuminate some dim story. He is there because he belongs.

OLIVIER: FILMOGRAPHY

TOO MANY CROOKS

1930

Production company: Fox. *Country:* G.B. *Running time:* 38 minutes. *Director:* George King. *Story by:* Basil Roscoe. *Screenplay by:* Billie Bristow.

CAST

Laurence Olivier . . . .*The Man*
Dorothy Boyd. . . . . *The Girl*
A. Bromley Davenport . . . .*The Man Upstairs*
Mina Burnett. . . . . *The Maid*
Arthur Stratton. . . . . *The Burglar*
Ellen Pollock. . . . .*Rose*

STORY

A young man is dared by his fiancée to burgle a certain mansion. While opening the safe, in the dead of the night, he is surprised first by a beautiful girl and then by a professional crook who takes the property which has been removed from the safe. With the arrival of the police and the tenant of the house, the latter is revealed as a spy with stolen plans, the girl as a member of the C.I.D., and the amateur cracksman as the actual owner of the house which he has entered merely to procure his passport.

CRITICS' CIRCLE

"Laurence Olivier's work on the screen has, up to the present time, been particularly limited, but if his future work is up to the standard he has set here, his appearance in the leading role of a more ambitious film is assured." — *Bioscope*

NOTES

Although *Bioscope* implies there may have been others, this was in fact Olivier's first film. It was a "quota quickie" made to satisfy rules limiting the number of American films that could be screened in Britain.

With Dorothy Boyd: debut of a romantic hero.

With Mina Burnett as the Maid.

THE TEMPORARY WIDOW

1930

Production company: Universum Film Aktiengesellschaft. *Distributed by:* Wardour. *Country:* G.B. and Germany. *Running time:* 84 minutes. *Producer:* Erich Pommer. *Director:* Gustav Ucicky. *Screenplay:* Karl Hartl, Walter Reisch and Benn Levy, *based upon the play "Hokuspokus" by:* Curt Goetz. *Photography:* Carl Hoffman. *Design:* Rohrig and Herlth.

CAST

Lilian Harvey . . . . *Kitty Kellermann*
Laurence Olivier . . . . *Peter Bille*
Felix Aylmer . . . . *The Public Prosecutor*
Frederick Lloyd . . . . *Counsel for the Defence*
Athole Stewart . . *President of the Court of Justice*
Fritz Schmuck . . . . *Councillor Hartmann*
Henry Caine . . . . *Councillor Lindberg*
Rene Hubert . . . . *Witness Loiret*
Frank Stanmore . . . . *Witness Kulicke*
Gillian Dean . . . . *Witness Anny Sedal*
Norman Williams . . . . *Auctioneer Kuhnen*
Stanley Lathburg . . . . *Valet John*
Johannes Roth . . . . *Master Mailor*
John Payne . . . . *Old Usher*
Erich Kestin . . . . *Young Usher*
Adolf Schroder . . . . *Soldier*
Danchell E. Hambro . . . . *Foreman of the Jury*
Ida Teater . . . . *Female Juror*
Oswald Skilbeck . . . . *First Juror*

STORY

Kitty Kellermann is being tried for the murder of her husband, an unsuccessful artist. The case for the prosecution is strong, the crime apparently having been committed some months previously by the accused upsetting a boat and leaving her husband to drown. Most of the action takes place in the courtroom as the circumstantial evidence against her mounts. After many witnesses, a man rises in court and confesses to the murder. It is the missing artist himself; the couple have tricked the public in order to enhance the value of his many unsold pictures.

CRITICS' CIRCLE

"Surprise ending. Brilliant acting. Good production. Extraordinary suspense values." — *Bioscope*

NOTES

Based on Curt Goetz's mystery play *Hokuspokus*, this film was made in simultaneous German- and English-language versions: Lilian Harvey played in both, but for the German version Olivier's character was played by Willy Fritsch. Reviewing this version, the *New York Times* referred to "whimsical curlycues of dialogue" and reckoned that the whole affair was light without becoming ridiculous. A footnote added that "the engaging young Englishman Lawrence Olivier" was in the English version. There is an extract from the Olivier version in *Elstree Story*, produced in 1952.

With Felix Aylmer (left) in the English-language version.

FRIENDS AND LOVERS

1931

Production company: RKO. *Country:* U.S.A. *Running time:* 66 minutes. *Director:* Victor Schertzinger. *Adapted by:* Jane Murfin, *from the novel "The Sphinx Has Spoken" by* Maurice de Kobra.

CAST

Adolphe Menjou . . . . *Captain Roberts*
Lily Damita. . . . . *Alva Sangrito*
Erich von Stroheim . . . . *Victor Sangrito*
Laurence Olivier . . . . *Lieut. Nichols*
Hugh Herbert . . . . *McNellis*
Frederick Kerr. . . . . *General Armstrong*
Blanche Friderici. . . . . *Lady Alice*
Yvonne D'Arcy . . . .*French Maid*
Dorothy Wolbert. . . . . *English Barmaid*
Kay Deslys . . . . *Waitress*

STORY

Alva is used by her husband to blackmail susceptible men. She falls in love with one of them, Capt. Roberts, but on Indian frontier duty he meets Lieut. Nichols, one of her earlier victims. They quarrel, but make it up, putting their friendship before love. Back in England their rivalry breaks out again, but in the end, after Alva's husband is shot, a scandal is avoided and Nichols urges Roberts to go away with Alva.

CRITICS' CIRCLE

"Laurence Olivier tends to be 'precious' as Nichols." — *Picturegoer*

POTIPHAR'S WIFE

(U.S. Title: HER STRANGE DESIRE)

1931

Production company: British International Pictures. *Distributed by:* First National Pathe. *Country:* G.B. *Running time:* 78 minutes. *Director:* Maurice Elvey. *Adapted by:* Edgar Middleton *from his own stage comedy.*

CAST

Laurence Olivier	*Straker*
Nora Swinburne	*Lady Diana Bromford*
Norman McKinnell	*Lord Bromford*
Guy Newall	*Hon. Maurice Worthington*
Donald Calthrop	*Counsel for Defence*
Ronald Frankau	*Maj. Tony Barlow*
Betty Schuster	*Rosita Worthington*
Marjorie Brooks	*Sylvia Barlow*
Walter Armitage	*Geoffrey Hayes*
Elsa Lanchester	*Therese*

STORY

Straker, a good-looking chauffeur employed by an aristocratic lady, is tempted by her towards an affair. His indifference arouses her wrath and he is charged with assault at the Assizes.

CRITICS' CIRCLE

"If it were not for Maurice Elvey's skilful handling of situations, the whole thing would be objectionable." — Lionel Collier, *Picturegoer*

With Nora Swinburne, Norman McKinnell and Walter Armitage.

THE YELLOW PASSPORT

(U.S. Title: THE YELLOW TICKET)

1931

Production company: Fox. Country: U.S.A. Running time: 75 minutes. *Director:* Raoul Walsh. *Screenplay:* Jules Furthman, Guy Bolton, *adapted from the play by:* Michael Morton. *Photography:* James Wong Howe. *Editor:* Jack Murray. *Sound recorder:* Donald Flick.

CAST

Elissa Landi . . . . *Marya Kalish*
Lionel Barrymore . . . . *Baron Andrey*
Laurence Olivier . . . . *Julian Rolphe*
Walter Byron . . . . *Prince Nicolai*
Sarah Padden . . . . *Mother Kalish*
Arnold Kroff . . . . *Grandfather Kalish*
Mischa Auer . . . . *Melchoer*
Boris Karloff . . . .*Orderly*
Rita La Roy . . . . *Fania*

STORY

Marya is a Jewish girl in Czarist Russia. She secures a yellow passport to allow her to travel to St. Petersburg where she believes her father is ill. There she learns her father has been killed and meets Rolphe, a British journalist who writes articles for the English and American newspapers. She tells him of the true facts, about the persecutions and murders carried out by the state, and he begins to write articles which bring him to the attention of the Secret Police, who have been persecuting Marya. When Baron Andrey, head of the Czar's secret police, learns of her persecution he gives her his travel documents but with the purpose of enticing her to his house. When he makes advances she shoots him and escapes with Rolphe to England.

CRITICS' CIRCLE

"Toward the end there are scenes in the British Embassy which are not a little exaggerated. Up to that time the story is a stirring one of its kind and Mr. Barrymore's work is especially intriguing. Laurence Olivier portrays Rolphe quite persuasively and Walter Byron gives a good account of himself as Count Nicolai, the Baron's dissolute nephew." — *N.Y. Times*

"If it were not for the acting of Elissa Landi and Lionel Barrymore, this picture would be of little entertainment value." — Lionel Collier, *Picturegoer Weekly*

NOTES

In this film Lionel Barrymore played the part his brother John had played on the stage in 1914.

With Elissa Landi as Marya.

With Lionel Barrymore as the Baron.

The romantic hero: with Elissa Landi in *The Yellow Passport.*

WESTWARD PASSAGE

1932

With Zasu Pitts as Mrs Truesdale.

Congratulations from Zasu Pitts for Olivier and Ann Harding.

Production company: RKO. *Country:* U.S.A. *Running time:* 72 minutes. *Director:* Robert Milton. *Adapted by* Robert Milton *from a novel by* Margaret Barnes.

CAST

Ann Harding	*Olivia Van Tyne*
Laurence Olivier	*Nick Allen*
Zasu Pitts	*Mrs. Truesdale*
Juliette Compton	*Henriette*
Irving Pichel	*Harry Lenman*
Irene Purcell	*Diane Van Tyne*
Julie Haydon	*Bridesmaid*
Joyce Compton	*Girl*
Emmett King	*Ottendorf*
Ethel Griffies	*Lady Coverly*
Nance O'Neil	*Mrs. Van Tyne*
Bonita Granville	*Little Olivia*

STORY

Olivia romantically marries Nick, an impoverished writer, but finds she cannot cope and poverty kills her love. They divorce and she marries Harry, an old friend, who accepts Nick's child as his own. Ten years later, happy in the more secure world of nannies, servants and tea parties, Olivia meets Nick again, now a very successful writer: he persuades her to try again, telling her that he has always loved her. She goes away with him but finds their lives still incompatible and returns to her husband.

CRITICS' CIRCLE

"Laurence Olivier, the English actor, fails to make an attractive character out of Nick Allen, the man who marries young and without means. The role should have been an expression of love's young dream as imagined by an impetuous and volatile lover. Instead Olivier tends to make him a 'bounder'." — Lionel Collier, *Picturegoer Weekly*

". . . effervescent characterisation by Olivier in rôle of poetically minded but impulsive author." — *The Cinema*

"Effervescence . . . and an attractive character", Olivier with Ann Harding.

NO FUNNY BUSINESS

1933

Public Lives: Olivier and Gertrude Lawrence.

Production company: John Stafford Productions. *Distributed by:* United Artists. *Country:* G.B. *Running time:* 75 minutes. *Producer:* John Stafford. *Directors:* John Stafford and Victor Hanbury. *Screenplay:* Victor Hanbury and Frank Vosper, *based on a story by* Dorothy Hope. *Photography:* W. Blakeley and D. Langley. *Editor:* Elmer McGovern.

CAST

Gertrude Lawrence . . . .*Yvonne*
Laurence Olivier . . . .*Clive*
Jill Esmond. . . . . *Anne*
Gibb McLaughlin. *Florey*
Edmond Breon . . . .*Edward*
Muriel Aked . . . . *Mrs. Fothergill*

STORY

Two employees of an enquiry agency (Anne and Clive) are sent as professional co-respondents to a hotel on the Riviera to meet a husband and wife who are there, unknown to each other, and who are half-heartedly considering a divorce. The pair meet, each mistaking the other for the client, fall in love, quarrel when their mistake is discovered, and are re-united. The husband and wife also meet and decide to stay married.

CRITICS' CIRCLE

"The story is complicated and slow, and the humour generally forced; so that one relies almost solely on the famous stage star (Gertrude Lawrence) for entertainment." — Lionel Collier, *Picturegoer*

"This comedy, with its stagey plot and sets, slow-developed situations and badly dated dialogue, has a certain fascination as a period piece. Gertrude Lawrence conveys a good deal of vitality and assurance, although playing in a manner long outmoded; Laurence Olivier, however, looks somewhat unhappy as the conventional juvenile lead of the period." — *Monthly Film Bulletin, June, 1951 (re-issue)*

NOTES

This film was re-issued in 1951 by Sun Film Distributors Ltd.

An English studio idea of the Riviera high life.

PERFECT UNDERSTANDING

1933

Supporting Gloria Swanson: "Star in difficult role".

With Nora Swinburne as Stephanie

Part of the "competent cast".

Production company: Gloria Swanson British. *Distributed by:* United Artists. *Country:* G.B. *Running time:* 79 minutes. *Director:* Cyril Gardner. *Screenplay:* Michael Powell. *Story by:* Miles Malleson. *Editor:* Thorold Dickinson.

CAST

Gloria Swanson	*Judy Rogers*
Laurence Olivier	*Nicholas Randall*
John Halliday	*Ronnson*
Sir Nigel Playfair	*Lord Portleigh*
Michael Farmer	*George*
Genevieve Tobin	*Kitty*
Nora Swinburne	*Stephanie*
Charles Cullum	*Sir John*
Peter Hawthorne	*Butler*
O. B. Clarence	*Dr. Graham*
Mary Jerrold	*Mrs. Graham*

STORY

Judy Rogers, an American girl visiting England, falls in love with Nicholas Randall. They decide to marry but to retain their individual freedom. After a lengthy honeymoon Judy returns to London to prepare their flat and Nick goes to Cannes where he is injured in a speed-boat race. He is taken to the villa owned by Stephanie, a young married woman who is in love with him, and he spends the night with her, which he confesses to Judy on his return. She retaliates by going to visit Ronnson, a secret admirer, although she doesn't break her marriage vows. She tells Nick she is expecting a child, and, suspicious, he asks for a divorce but then changes his mind in the nick of time.

CRITICS' CIRCLE

"Deft treatment of not too convincing material provides entertaining sequence of amusing, dramatic, exciting and emotional incidents with motor boat race and divorce procedures as highlights. Very capable direction reveals touches of subtlety and illuminating detail. Sophisticated dialogue dominating factor of sincere attempt to solve marriage problems. Very well acted by competent cast with admirable portrayal by star in difficult role." — *The Cinema Booking Guide Supplement*, April, 1933

Olivier in the best of the moustaches.

MOSCOW NIGHTS
(U.S. Title: I STAND CONDEMNED)

1935

Production company: London Films — Capitol. *Distributed by:* General Film Distributors. *Country:* G.B. *Running time:* 76 minutes. *Producers:* Alexander Korda, Alexis Granowski, Max Schach. *Director:* Anthony Asquith. *Screenplay:* Erich Siepmann, *adapted from the novel "Les Nuits De Moscou" by* Pierre Benoit. *Photography:* Philip Tannura. *Recording director:* A. W. Watkins. *Assistant director:* Edward Baird. *Film editor:* Francis B. Lyon. *Supervising editor:* William Hernbeck.

CAST
Harry Baur . . . .*Brioukow*
Laurence Olivier . . . . *Ignatoff*
Penelope Dudley Ward . . . . *Natasha*
Robert Cochran. *Polonsky*
Morton Selten . . . . *Kovrin*
Athene Seyler . . . .*Madame Sabline*
Walter Hudd . . . .*The Doctor*
Kate Cutler . . . . *Madame Kovrin*
Charles Hallard . . . . *President of the Court Martial*
Edmund Willard . . . . . .*Officer for the Prosecution*
Charles Carson. . . . . *Officer for the Defence*
Morland Graham . . . .*Brioukow's servant*
Hay Petrie . . . . *The Spy*

STORY
The story is set in Russia in 1916. Natasha, a Russian society girl, is persuaded by her impoverished parents to become engaged to Brioukow, a wealthy middle-aged contractor. While working in a hospital she falls in love with Ignatoff but remains faithful to Brioukow. Brioukow is still jealous and goads Ignatoff into running up gambling debts which he has no means of paying until Madame Sabline gives him the money. Madame Sabline is proved a spy and Ignatoff is arrested as her accomplice. Brioukow has evidence which he uses to free Ignatoff even though it costs him Natasha.

CRITICS' CIRCLE
"The situations in the story are not original, but the treatment throughout is excellent and Mr. Asquith must be complimented on almost every ground." — *Sunday Times*

"For those who think as I do that it is a bad film, there is one consolation. The original, which it was possible to see in Paris eight months ago, was far, far worse . . . But the surprise of the picture is Laurence Olivier, who plays the young officer with as much wit and feeling as if the tom-fool fellow were really a possible character. Such pleasure as I got from *Moscow Nights* was largely due to Mr. Olivier's recurrent appearances on the screen." — *The Observer*

NOTES
There was a re-issue of this film in 1942 by Pioneer Exclusives.

With Penelope Dudley Ward, who later married the director Carol Reed.

CRITICS' CIRCLE

"Of its kind, *Lady X* is a pleasant enough picture, lifted out of the nitwit class by the acting of Olivier and still more by Ralph Richardson." — *New Statesman*

"Merle Oberon is delightfully natural and eminently desirable as Leslie and Laurence Olivier is polished and refreshingly human as Logan, but the player who steals the picture is Ralph Richardson." — *Kinematograph Weekly*

"It's never exceptionally complicated — just the story of Merle Oberon twisting Olivier prettily around her little finger — but the excellent acting and Tim Whelan's smooth resourceful direction give it wit, distinction, and body ... Laurence Olivier is in unusually good form and gives what is his best screen performance yet..." — *Film Weekly*

NOTES

This film was re-issued in 1944 by Ealing Distributors. It was an early Technicolor film and the notices reflected that novelty.

With Ralph Richardson and Binnie Barnes.

Q PLANES
(U.S. Title: CLOUDS OVER EUROPE)

1939

Production company: Harefield — London Films. *Distributed by:* Columbia. *Country:* G.B. *Running time:* 82 minutes. *Producer:* Irving Asher, Alexander Korda. *Director:* Tim Whelan. *Story by:* Brock Williams, Jack Whittingham and Arthur Wimperis. *Screenplay:* Ian Dalrymple. *Photography:* Harry Stradling. *Supervising art editor:* Vincent Korda. *Supervising editor:* William Hornbeck. *Recording director:* W. W. Watkins. *Musical director:* Muir Mathieson. *Film editor:* Hugh Stewart. *Assistant art director:* Frederick Pusey.

CAST

Laurence Olivier . . . .*Tony McVane*
Ralph Richardson . . . . *Major Hammond*
Valerie Hobson . . . . *Kay*
George Curzon . . . .*Jenkins*
George Merritt. . . . .*Barrett*
Gus McNaughton. . . . .*Blenkinsop*
David Tree. . . . .*Mackenzie*
Sandra Storme. . . . .*Daphne*
Hay Petrie . . . .*Stage Door Keeper*
Frank Fox. . . . . *Karl*
George Butler . . . . *Air Marshall Gosport*
Gordon McLeod . . . . *The Baron*
John Longden . . . .*Peters*
Reginald Purdell . . . .*Pilot*
John Laurie. . . . .*Editor*
Pat Aherne . . . . *Officer*

STORY

Tony McVane is a dashing test pilot but the aeroplane factory he tests for has had a number of planes disappear. Through the connivings of Jenkins, the confidential secretary to the factory manager, they have been secreted onto a ship during their test flights. Olivier is likewise captured but fights free while Hammond from Scotland Yard comes to the rescue with a destroyer.

CRITICS' CIRCLE

"... it is rousing espionage, romantic melodrama, staged in the best happy-go-lucky but pukka British tradition ... Ralph Richardson displays infectious humour as the easy-going alcoholic Hammond, yet never loses a sense of character. There are brains behind his fooling. Laurence Olivier and Valerie Hobson are natural as Tony and Kay." — *Kinematograph Weekly*

"Despite its subject, *Q Planes* is mainly a comedy — a sort of *Thin Man* in an espionage setting.... Much of its success is due to Ralph Richardson, who cleverly holds together the comedy and dramatic ingredients as Major Hammond. . . . Olivier is good, as always, as one of the test pilots and Valerie Hobson provides the necessary romance interest as a girl reporter with whom he falls in love." — Lionel Collier, *Picturegoer*

"Laurence Olivier has comparatively little to do beyond look virile and masculine as the nominal hero of the piece and Valerie Hobson lends her compensating charm to one of those phoney girl-reporter roles." — *Film Weekly*

NOTES
This film was re-issued in 1944 by Key Distributors.

Future knights of the English theatre at the start of a long partnership.

"Little to do beyond looking virile and masculine".

With Valerie Hobson as Kay: "a sort of *Thin Man* in an espionage setting".

"Brains behind the fooling".

WUTHERING HEIGHTS

1939

A Samuel Goldwyn Presentation. *Released through:* United Artists. *Country:* U.S.A. *Running time:* 104 minutes. *Producer:* Samuel Goldwyn. *Director:* William Wyler. *Screenplay:* Ben Hecht and Charles MacArthur, *based on the novel by:* Emily Brontë. *Photography:* Gregg Toland. *Art director:* James Basevi. *Set decorator:* Julia Heron. *Musical director:* Alfred Newman. *Costume designer:* Omar Kiam. *Film editor:* Daniel Mandell. *Sound recorder:* Paul Heal. *Assistant director:* Walter Mayo. *Special character make-up:* Blagoe Stephanoff.

CAST

Merle Oberon . . . . *Cathy*
Laurence Olivier . . . . *Heathcliff*
David Niven. . . . . *Edgar Linton*
Flora Robson . . . . *Ellen Dean*
Donald Crisp . . . . *Dr. Kenneth*
Hugh Williams . . . . *Hindley*
Geraldine Fitzgerald . . . . *Isabella*
Leo G. Carroll . . . . *Joseph*
Cecil Humphreys. . . . . *Judge Linton*
Miles Mander. . . . . *Lockwood*
Romaine Callender . . . . *Robert*
Cecil Kellaway. . . . . *Earnshaw*
Rex Downing . . . . *Heathcliff (as child)*
Sarita Wooton . . . . *Cathy (as child)*
Douglas Scott . . . . *Hindley (as child)*

STORY

Lockwood, the new tenant of The Grange, spends an eerie and snowbound night at Wuthering Heights, the home of Heathcliff, his neighbour. The next day, on his return, Ellen, the housekeeper, tells him the story of the house and its ghosts. Ellen was once housekeeper at Wuthering Heights to Mr. Earnshaw, a widower with two children, Cathy and Hindley. Earnshaw adopted a starving gypsy boy he found on the streets and called him Heathcliff. Heathcliff and Cathy became constant companions. When Hindley became master of the house on Earnshaw's death he put Heathcliff, of whom he had always been jealous, out of the house and forced him to work as a stable boy. Hindley turned to drink and as they grew older Heathcliff and Cathy turned to each other. Companionship became love, and though she urged him not to put up with her brother's ill-treatment of him, Heathcliff preferred to stay near Cathy. Due to a misunderstanding, Heathcliff left and eventually Cathy married the polished and urbane Edgar Linton of The Grange. Heathcliff returned from America very wealthy and bought Wuthering Heights. As revenge for Cathy's marriage, Heathcliff married her sister-in-law and treated her very badly. He was still in love, passionately, with Cathy and she with him. Cathy died in Heathcliff's arms and he begged her to haunt him.

CRITICS' CIRCLE

"This Heathcliff would never have married for revenge. Mr. Olivier's nervous, breaking voice belongs to balconies and Verona and romantic love." — Graham Greene, *New Statesman*

"Laurence Olivier makes a fine, cryptic and dominant job of Heathcliff and Merle Oberon opposite him gets over the difficulties of being beautiful, wild and sweet all at once very well. The only fault with the picture as a whole, though, is that these people are not in themselves twisted enough to make their actions and end inevitable: they are able to give credence to a scene once they are in it, but they have not by intrinsic nature prepared you for the revelations of such dark obsessions." — Otis Ferguson, *The New Republic*

"Laurence Olivier puts over a magnificent performance as Heathcliff. The character seldom deserves sympathy, while the transformation from clod to man of wealth and vengeance is, to say the least, fantastic, but he not only brings conviction to his portrayal but translates intelligently its mystical quality." — *Kinematograph Weekly*

"Distinguished by earnest performances, telling direction and intelligent writing, this studious pic-

"Haunt me, Cathy": Olivier with Merle Oberon on Hollywood's moors.

turisation of the early Victorian novel by Emily Brontë is typical of Samuel Goldwyn production at its polished best." — *Motion Picture Herald*

"The pair chosen for the lovers have done all but magnificently. Not being Irving, Chaliapin and Conrad Veidt all rolled into one, Mr. Laurence Olivier does not give a superhuman performance. But the performance he does give is extremely good and suggests what I take to be very important, that somewhere in Heathcliff's dark soul there is a spot of something which in another world or dimension might grow to compunction. Or shall I put it that in this film Mr. Olivier acts best when he acts least and that he superbly portrays the dumb agony which the gipsy has in common with his animals." — James Agate, *The Tatler*

NOTES

It has become part of Hollywood legend that there was a great deal of friction between Olivier and Miss Oberon during the filming of this picture. It was however this film (and particularly its director William Wyler) that made Olivier realise that movies were a medium potentially as important as the stage. After filming was finished and everyone had left, Sam Goldwyn ordered Wyler to shoot a new ending. "I don't want to look at a corpse at the fadeout," he said. He wanted to see the lovers re-united in heaven. Wyler refused, but Goldwyn had someone else make the shot — a double exposure of Olivier's stunt double and a girl seen walking on clouds.

Wuthering Heights (billed as "the strangest love story ever told") won the New York Critics' Award for Best Picture. It also won an Academy Award for Black and White Cinematography and Laurence Olivier (who had been cast after an unsuccessful test by Robert Newton) was nominated as Best Actor, 1939; but the Oscar was won by Robert Donat for *Goodbye Mr. Chips.*

"Looking back," said Olivier later, "I was snobbish about films ... but gradually I came to see that film was a different medium and that if one treated it as such, and tried to learn it, humbly, and with an open mind, one could work in it. I saw that it could use the best that was going ... it was Wyler who gave me the simple thought — if you do it right, you can do anything. And if he hadn't said that, I think I wouldn't have done *Henry V* five years later."

I am torn with *Desire* -- tortured by hate!

SAMUEL GOLDWYN
presents

WUTHERING HEIGHTS

co-starring

MERLE OBERON · LAURENCE OLIVIER · DAVID NIVEN
with FLORA ROBSON · DONALD CRISP · GERALDINE FITZGERALD · Released thru UNITED ARTISTS
Directed by WILLIAM WYLER

Heathcliff returns: Merle Oberon (seated) and David Niven (far right).

PRIDE AND PREJUDICE

1940

Production company: M.G.M. *Distributed by:* M.G.M. *Country:* U.S.A. *Running time:* 118 minutes. *Producer:* Hunt Stromberg. *Director:* Robert Z. Leonard. *Screenplay:* Aldous Huxley and Jane Murfin, *based on the dramatisation of Jane Austen's novel by:* Helen Jerome. *Technical adviser:* George Richelavie. *Photography:* Karl Freund. *Musical score:* Herbert Stothart. *Recording:* Douglas Shearer. *Art director:* Cedric Gibbons. *Art associate:* Paul Groesse. *Set decoration:* Edwin B. Willis. *Gowns:* Adrian. *Dance director:* Ernst Matray. *Film editor:* Robert J. Kern.

CAST

Those living at Meryton Village
Edward Ashley . . . . *Mr. Wickham*
Merton Lamont. . . . . *Mr. Denny*
E. E. Clive . . . . *Sir William Lucas*
Marjorie Wood. . . . .*Lady Lucas*
May Beatty . . . .*Mrs. Philips*
Those living at Longbourn
Greer Garson. . . . . *Elizabeth Bennet*
Maureen O'Sullivan . . . . *Jane Bennet*
Ann Rutherford . . . . *Lydia Bennet*
Marsha Hunt . . . .*Mary Bennet*
Heather Angel . . . . *Kitty Bennet*
Mary Boland . . . . *Mrs. Bennet*
Edmund Gwenn . . . .*Mr. Bennet*
Those living at Netherfield
Laurence Olivier . . . .*Mr. Darcy*
Frieda Inescort . . . . *Miss Bingley*
Bruce Lester . . . .*Mr. Bingley*
Those living at Rosings
Edna May Oliver . . . . . . *Lady Catherine de Bourgh*
Gia Kent . . . . *Anne de Bourgh*
Melville Cooper . . . . *Mr. Collins*
Karen Morley . . . . *Mrs. Collins*

STORY

Mr. Bennet is a gentleman in the best sense of the word, while his wife has the triple misfortune of being the daughter of a shopkeeper, the sister of an attorney and a naturally vulgar woman who can't keep her mouth shut. The personality and clever-

With Frieda Inescort and Bruce Lester.

With Edna May Oliver and Gia Kent.

With director Robert Z. Leonard (seated left) during a break in shooting.

ness of her daughter Elizabeth and the beauty of her daughter Jane attract two rich and distinguished bachelors, Darcy and Bingley. But Darcy is proud of his noble birth and connections and feels that he must not love Elizabeth nor permit his friend to marry Jane. There is nothing against the two girls but that the family is 'common'.

Elizabeth feels the pride in Darcy and turns against him, bringing about a battle which ends with Darcy's capitulation. Elizabeth refuses to marry him but she relents and agrees when Darcy not only patches up the romance between Jane and Bingley but also gives her youngest sister Lydia a large dowry to entice into marriage the adventurer she has run away with.

CRITICS' CIRCLE

"Olivier makes a fine, contemptuous, gradually unbending Darcy." — *New Statesman*

"... *Pride and Prejudice* at times achieves a close resemblance to the book of the same name. Both Greer Garson as Elizabeth and Laurence Olivier as Darcy breathe the original zephyrs in several scenes." — Basil Wright, *The Spectator*

With Greer Garson and Melville Cooper.

Garson, Olivier, director Robert D. Leonard and the *Pride and Prejudice* unit.

LADY HAMILTON
(U.S. Title: THAT HAMILTON WOMAN)

1941

Production company: Alexander Korda Films. *Released by:* United Artists. Ealing Distributors. *Country:* U.S.A./G.B. *Running time:* 125 minutes. *Producer and director:* Alexander Korda. *Screenplay:* Walter Reisch and R. C. Sheriff. *Art director:* Vincent Korda. *Associate:* Lyle Reynolds Wheeler. *Photography:* Rudolph Mate. *Costumes:* Rene Hubert. *Musical director:* Miklos Rozsa. *Special effects:* Laurence Butler. *Special sequences photographed by:* Edward Linden. *Set decorations:* Julia Heron. *Editor:* William Hornbeck. *Sound technician:* William H. Wilmarth. *Make-up artist:* Blagoe Stephanoff.

CAST

Vivien Leigh . . . .*Emma, Lady Hamilton*
Laurence Olivier . . . . *Lord Nelson*
Alan Mowbray. . . . . *Sir William Hamilton*
Sara Allgood . . . . *Mrs. Cadogan-Lyon*
Gladys Cooper. . . . .*Lady Nelson*
Henry Wilcoxon . . . . *Captain Hardy*
Heather Angel . . . .*A Street Girl*
Halliwell Hobbes . . . . , *Reverend Nelson*
Gilbert Emery . . . . *Lord Spencer*
Miles Mander. *Lord Keith*
Ronald Sinclair . . . .*Josiah*
Luis Alberni . . . . *King of Naples*
Norma Drury. . . . .*Queen of Naples*
Olaf Hytten. . . . . *Gavin*
Juliette Compton . . . . *Lady Spencer*
Guy Kingsford. . . . . *Captain Troubridge*

STORY

In 1786 Emma Hart arrives at the British Embassy in Naples expecting to marry the nephew of the Ambassador, Sir William Hamilton — but she learns she has been used as a pawn in the marriage plans. Instead, Sir William falls in love with her and marries her, despite her questionable reputation. In 1793 Captain Horatio Nelson meets her as he is recruiting Italian soldiers in the war against Napoleon. Lady Hamilton, an intimate of the Queen, gets him twice the number he has requested. They meet again in 1798 and become closer. Revolution breaks out in Naples and, against orders, Nelson returns to England but, with Emma, is in the midst of scandal. She has a child in secret and sends it away to the country. She and Nelson plan retirement to the country but Nelson is killed at Trafalgar and she is left alone.

CRITICS' CIRCLE

"The death scene is finely done, a moving piece of acting. Laurence Olivier's performance as Nelson, indeed, is within its conventions good throughout." — Dilys Powell, *Sunday Times*

"Mr. Churchill has seen this film eleven times since it first appeared in 1941 ... Vivien Leigh and Laurence Olivier are dressed like Nelson and Lady Hamilton, they go through all the joys which beset that not so ill-fated couple, but they are seldom other than two modern film stars led in and out of the scenes by the accepted clichés." — Richard Winnington, *News Chronicle*

"The picture has distinct topical appeal in its parallel with the events of today, when once more a

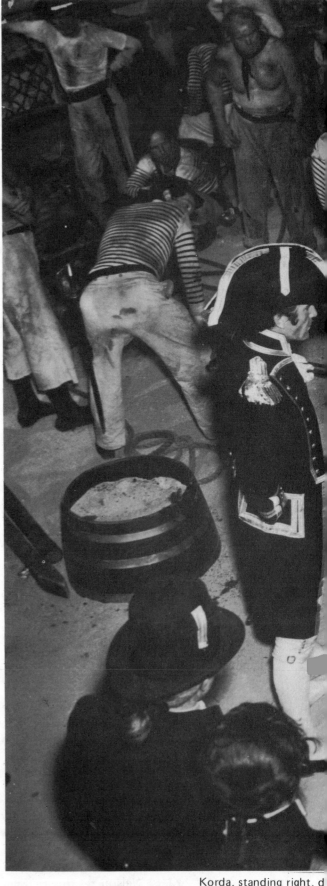

tyrant strives to dominate the world, and England again stands in his way. The portrayal, too, is finely satisfying, with Vivien Leigh giving a brilliantly sympathetic performance in the title role and Laurence Olivier a finely dignified figure of our greatest sailor." — *Today's Cinema*

"*Lady Hamilton* is a good entertainment film, with unusually good acting in all parts. The settings are also good, with the rather serious exception of the battle of Trafalgar, which is — perhaps unavoidably — quite comic in its unreality ... Historically the film is worthless." — Dr. Rachel Reid of The Historical Association, *Sight and Sound*

NOTES
This film was re-released in 1941, 1944 and 1948.

Korda, standing right, d

90

in the "Kiss Me Hardy" sequence at Trafalgar. Henry Wilcoxon, as Hardy, is standing left.

49th PARALLEL

(U.S. Title: THE INVADERS)

1941

Production company: Ortus Films. General Film Distributors Ltd. *Country:* G.B. *Running time:* 123 minutes. *Producers:* Michael Powell and John Sutro. *Director:* Michael Powell. *Original story and screenplay:* Emeric Pressburger. *Scenario by:* Rodney Ackland and Emeric Pressburger. *Editor:* David Lean. *Photography:* Frederick Young. *In charge of production:* Harold Boxall. *Associates:* Ronald Gillett and George Brown. *Art director:* David Rawnsley. *Canadian adviser:* Nugent M. Cloucher. *Sound supervision:* A. W. Watkins. *Associate director:* A. Seabourne. *Associate editor:* Hugh Stewart. *Continuity:* Betty Curtis. *Musical score composed by:* Ralph Vaughan Williams. *Musical director:* Muir Mathieson with the London Symphony Orchestra.

CAST

The U Boat Crew

Richard George . . . . *Kommandant Bernsdorff*
Eric Portman. . . . . *Lieutenant Hirth*
Raymond Lovell . . . . *Lieutenant Kuhnecke*
Niall MacGinnis. . . . . *Vogel*
Peter Moore. . . . . *Kranz*
John Chandos . . . . *Lohrmann*
Basil Appleby . . . . *Jahner*

The Canadians

Laurence Olivier . . . . *Johnnie, the Trapper*
Finlay Currie. . . . . *The Factor*
Ley On . . . . *Nick, the Eskimo*
Anton Walbrook . . . . *Peter*
Glynis Johns . . . . *Anna*
Charles Victor . . . . *Andreas*
Frederick Piper . . . . *David*
Leslie Howard . . . . *Philip Armstrong Scott*
Tawera Moana. . . . . *George, the Indian*
Eric Clavering . . . . *Art*
Charles Rolfe. . . . . *Bob*
Raymond Massey . . . . *Andy Brock*
Theodore Salt and O. W. Fonger .*The U.S. Customs Officers*

STORY

Six Nazis are stranded on the North coast of Canada when their U-Boat is destroyed by Royal Canadian Air Force bombers. The Nazis take over an Eskimo village and shoot Johnnie, the French trapper, when he tries to summon help over the short-wave radio. The six then set off across Canada towards Vancouver and one by one are killed until only Hirth is left in a desperate attempt to reach the U.S. which is as yet not involved in the war. He is recognized by Andy who thwarts his escape attempt.

CRITICS' CIRCLE

"A famous cast interprets the leading roles with a perfection of light and shade that keeps the theme in perspective and gives an irresistible force to speech and action . . . To our mind, the most appealing of the roles is that of the French Canadian trapper played by Laurence Olivier, for he breaks away from the convention and gives a plain study of a simple soul aghast at the vicious cruelty of the Nazi doctrines and their adherents, incomprehending the politics of the war but ready to die for his faith." — *Today's Cinema*

"This is the first British feature film to be inspired and partly financed by an official government body — the Ministry of Information, to be exact. It's production was whitened with the dust of trade conflict, and for a time it looked as though there would be no film, but only a nasty smell. But *49th Parallel* was completed and has had one of the best presses ever accorded to a British production. It is, moreover, one of the few films of a purely episodic nature which has ever come off." — *Documentary News Letter*

NOTES

This film was made in Montreal (Associated Sound Studios) and at Denham, England.

It was the first film to be commissioned by the Ministry of Information in 1940 and was an enormous commercial success, earning back its entire production cost in three months in the United Kingdom. It was also the first film to commission a Vaughan Williams score. Olivier had only ten minutes of screen time and was, like all the cast, on half-pay.

Olivier as the Trapper, with Ley On as the Eskimo.

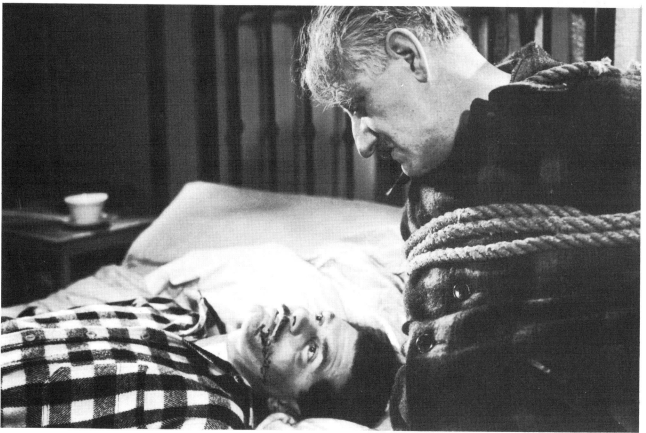

With Finlay Currie as the Factor.

THE DEMI-PARADISE
(U.S. Title: ADVENTURE FOR TWO)

1943

Production company: A Two Cities Film. General Film Distributors Ltd. *Country:* G.B. *Running time:* 115 minutes. *Produced and written by:* Anatole de Grunwald. *Director:* Anthony Asquith. *Photography:* Bernard Knowles. *Supervising art director:* Paul Sheriff. *Supervising editor:* Jack Harris. *Assistant to producer:* Gordon Parry. *Production manager:* Herbert Smith. *Assistant director:* George Pollock. *Art director:* Carmen Dillon. *Sound recordist:* J. C. Cook. *Editor:* Renee Woods. *Sound editor:* Harry Miller. *Recording director:* A. W. Watkins. *Music:* Nicholas Brodszky. *Musical direction:* Muir Mathieson.

CAST

Laurence Olivier . . *Ivan Dimitrievitch Kouznetsoff*
Penelope Dudley Ward . . . .*Ann Tisdall*
Marjorie Fielding. . . . . *Mrs. Tisdall*
Margaret Rutherford . . . . *Rowena Ventnor*
Felix Aylmer. . . . . *Mr. Runalow*
George Thorpe . . . .*Mr. Herbert Tisdall*
Leslie Henson . . . . *Leslie Henson*
Guy Middleton . . . .*Richard Christie*
Michael Shepley . . . . *Mr. Walford*
Edie Martin . . *Miss Winnifred Tisdall (Aunt Winnie)*
Muriel Aked . . . . *Mrs. Tisdall-Stanton*
Joyce Grenfell. . . . . *Mrs. Pawson*
Jack Watling . . . . *Tom Sellars*
Everley Gregg . . . . *Mrs. Flannel*
Aubrey Mallalieu. . . . . *Toomes, the Butler*
Brian Nissen . . . . *George Tisdall*
John Schofield . . . . *Ernie*
David Kerr. . . . . *Mr. Jordan*
Miles Malleson. . . . . *Box Office Manager*
John Laurie and John Boxer . . . . *British sailors*
Marian Spencer . . . . *Mrs. Teddy Beckett*
Margaret Withers . . . .*Mrs. Elliston*
Josephine Middleton . . . .*Mrs. Tremlow*
Beatrice Harrison. . . . . *Beatrice Harrison*
Inge Perten . . . .*Russian Doctor*
Wilfred Hyde White. . . . . *A waiter*
Alexis Chesnakoff . . . .*Russian delegate*
Mavis Clair. . . . . *Barmaid*
Charles Paton . . . . *Mr. Bishop*
George Street and Ben Williams. . . . .*Hecklers*

STORY

Ivan Dimitrievitch Kouznetsoff is a young Russian engineer, the inventor of a new propeller for ice breakers, who arrives in England in 1939, before the beginning of the war, and encounters a bewildering set of conventions and seeming petty-mindedness. Ann Tisdall takes him under her wing and she then tries to explain him to her family. He comes again in 1941 and finds the same dubious people and the same cautious spirit, but he begins to understand. At the end of his stay he is convinced of the possibility of Anglo-Soviet friendship.

CRITICS' CIRCLE

"The film drew a picture, ironic and yet at the same time affectionate, of English foibles. The visitor encounters all the surface idiosyncrasies of a reserved people: the unwelcoming landlady, the silent railway travellers, the apparent coldness and the casualness and suspicion of the average Englishman towards a foreigner. The Russian is chilled and discouraged until, with the entry of his country into the war against Germany, the genuine warmth and friendliness underlying British reserve come into play. *The Demi-Paradise* has innumerable touches of pictorial satire . . . (it) is remarkable too for the beautiful performance of Laurence Olivier as the bewildered Russian, a performance which put him for the first time in the top flight of British film actors." — Dilys Powell, *Films Since 1939*

"It *(The Demi-Paradise)* is occasionally tender, sometimes funny, oftener not so funny, strictly parochial and incurably olde-worlde, and we had probably better keep it to ourselves as a private unexportable joke. . . . I have no means of telling whether Laurence Olivier, who plays the Soviet engineer with a moody charm and a patiently sustained accent, is precisely what they ordered in Nijny-Petrovsk, but I have little doubt that the British characters . . . would be more quickly recognised in Shaftesbury Avenue than in Portsmouth, Clydeside or Hull." — C. A. Lejeune, *The Observer*

"The film is made by a dazzling performance from Laurence Olivier and the skilled direction of Anthony Asquith." — *New Statesman and Nation*

Instructions (on the English way of life as reflected in its postcards) from Penelope Dudley Ward.

HENRY V

1944

Laurence Olivier's presentation of a Two Cities Film. *Released by:* United Artists (U.S.A.). *Country:* G.B. Technicolor. *Running time:* 137 minutes. *Produced and directed by:* Laurence Olivier. *Editor:* Reginald Beck. *Art director:* Paul Sheriff. *Assistant art director:* Carmen Dillon. *Costume designer:* Roger Furse. *Assistant costume designer:* Margaret Furse. *Associate producer:* Dallas Bower. *Text editor:* Alan Dent. *Photography:* Robert Krasker. *Operating cameraman:* Jack Hildyard. *Sound recordists:* John Dennis and Desmond Dew. *Music:* William Walton. *Conducted by:* Muir Mathieson. *Played by:* The London Symphony Orchestra.

CAST

Laurence Olivier	*King Henry V*
Robert Newton	*Ancient Pistol*
Renée Asherson	*Princess Katharine*
Leslie Banks	*Chorus*
Esmond Knight	*Fluellen*
Leo Genn	*The Constable of France*
Felix Aylmer	*Archbishop of Canterbury*
Ralph Truman	*Mountjoy, the French Herald*
Nicholas Hannen	*Duke of Exeter*
Harcourt Williams	*King Charles VI of France*
Robert Helpmann	*Bishop of Ely*
Ivy StHelier	*Alice, Lady in Waiting*
Freda Jackson	*Mistress Quickly*
Ernest Thesiger	*Duke of Beri*
Jimmy Hanley	*Soldier in the English camp*
Max Adrian	*The Dauphin*
Niall MacGinnis	*Captain in the English army*
Valentine Dyall	*Duke of Burgundy*
George Robey	*Sir John Falstaff*
Russell Thorndike	*Duke of Bourbon*
Roy Emerton	*Lieutenant Bardolph*
Michael Shepley	*Gower*
Griffith Jones	*Earl of Salisbury*
Morland Graham	*Sir Thomas Erpingham*
Arthur Hambling	*Soldier in the English camp*
Brian Nissen	*Soldier in the English camp*
Frederick Cooper	*Corporal Nym*
Gerald Case	*Earl of Westmoreland*
Michael Warre	*Duke of Gloucester*
Janet Burnell	*Queen Isabel of France*
Frank Tickle	*Governor of Harfleur*
George Cole	*Boy*
Jonathan Field	*French Messenger*
Vernon Greeves	*English Herald*
Ernest Hare	*A Priest*

STORY

William Shakespeare's story of *Henry V*, his wooing

"A good heart , Kate, is the sun and the moon": Olivier, Asherson, StHelier

of Princess Katharine, the call to battle and the defeat of the French at the battle of Agincourt.

CRITICS' CIRCLE
"Laurence Olivier produces, directs and stars in *Henry V*. He deserves credit for undertaking the most ambitious film of our time. But it is also the most difficult, annoying, beautiful, boring, exciting, wordy, baffling picture yet made. It has a sort of damnable excellence." — Ernest Betts, *The People*

"In over-bright Technicolor, half an hour too long, at its worst it is vulgar and obscure, but at its best it is an indication of what could be done with Shakespeare on the screen." — Richard Winnington, *News Chronicle*

"At last there has been brought to the screen, with such sweetness, vigor, insight and beauty that it seemed to have been written yesterday, a play by the greatest dramatic poet who ever lived." — *Time*

"Tremendously exciting film that puts Shakespeare on screen with infinitely more success than any previous attempts have done or than I for one thought possible." — Matthew Norgate, *BBC*

"It is not, I repeat, the most exciting or inspiring or original film that I have seen. But I cannot think of any that seems to be more beautiful, more skilfully and charmingly achieved within its wisely ordered limits, or more thoroughly satisfying." — James Agee, *The Nation*

NOTES
Olivier felt the time was right for this patriotic film and tried to convince William Wyler (who had directed him in *Wuthering Heights*) to direct it. When Wyler refused and said "do it yourself", Olivier did just that. Originally he had hoped that Vivien Leigh would play Princess Katharine, but Selznick refused to release her on the grounds that the smallness of the part would "devalue" his Scarlett O'Hara.

Henry V ran for 46 weeks in New York, the longest run of any British film until that time, and it was judged the "best imported film of the year". In London it ran for five months at the Carlton, Haymarket.

Laurence Olivier won a special Academy Award in 1946 for "outstanding achievement as an actor, producer and director in bringing *Henry V* to the screen". The film also won one of the New York Critics' Awards for 1946. Yet a poll of "Money-Making Stars", by the *Motion Picture Herald* that year, placed Olivier behind James Mason, David Niven, George Formby and Eric Portman.

Before the battle: Olivier with Morland Graham as Erpingham.

On stage at the Globe: Leslie Banks (left), Olivier, Aylmer and Asherson.

"God for Harry, England and St George!"

HAMLET

1948

Laurence Olivier presents a Two Cities Film. *Distributed by:* General Film Distributors and J. Arthur Rank. *Country:* G.B. *Running time:* 2 hours 35 minutes. *Produced and directed by:* Laurence Olivier. *Designer:* Roger Furse. *Associate Producer:* Reginald Beck. *Photography:* Desmond Dickinson. *Art director:* Carmen Dillon. *Text editor:* Alan Dent. *Production supervisor:* Phil C. Samuel. *Assistant producer:* Anthony Bushell. *Editor:* Helga Cranston. *Production manager:* John Gossage. *Sound recorders:* John Mitchell and L. E. Overton. *Sound editor:* Harry Miller. *Assistant director:* Peter Bolton. *Special effects:* Paul Sheriff, Henry Harris and Jack Whitehead. *Mime play:* David Paltenghi. *Sword play:* Dennis Loraine. *Make-up:* Tony S. Forzini. *Hairdressing:* Vivienne Walker. *Set dresser:* Roger Ramsdell. *Music:* William Walton. *Conducted by:* Muir Mathieson. *Played by:* The Philharmonia Orchestra.

CAST

The Royal Court of Denmark
Eileen Herlie . . . .*Gertrude, the Queen*
Basil Sydney . . . . *Claudius, the King*
Laurence Olivier . . . . . *Hamlet, Prince of Denmark*
Norman Wooland . . . . *Horatio, his friend*
Felix Aylmer . . . .*Polonius, Lord Chamberlain*
Terence Morgan. . . . .*Laertes, his son*
Jean Simmons . . . . *Ophelia, his daughter*

Servants to the Court
Peter Cushing . . . .*Osric*
Stanley Holloway . . . . *Gravedigger*
Russell Thorndike . . . .*Priest*

Men at Arms
John Laurie. . . . .*Francisco*
Esmond Knight. . . . . *Bernardo*
Anthony Quayle . . . . *Marcellus*
Niall MacGinnis. . . . . *Sea Captain*

The Play within a Play
Harcourt Williams . . . .*First player*
Patrick Troughton. . . . . *Player King*
Tony Tarver . . . . *Player Queen*

STORY
William Shakespeare's tale of revenge and intrigue at Elsinore. Hamlet swears to his father's ghost to avenge his murder at the hands of Claudius, his uncle, who has now married his mother, Gertrude.

CRITICS' CIRCLE
"Hamlet" proves to be a study in simplification, a handsomely illustrated, handily abridged text-book for the general (public)" — C. A. Lejeune, *Observer*

"A man who can do what Laurence Olivier does for Shakespeare (and for those who treasure or will yet to learn to treasure Shakespeare) is certainly among the more valuable men of his time. In the strict sense, his films are not creative works of cinematic art: the essential art of moving pictures is overwhelmingly visual. But Olivier's films set up an equilateral triangle between the screen, stage and literature. And between the screen, stage and literature they establish an interplay, a shimmering splendour, of the disciplined vitality which is art . . . This one (*Hamlet*) in every piece of casting, in every performance, is about as nearly solid as gold can be . . . The most moving and gratifying thing in this film is to watch this talented artist, in the height of his accomplishment, work at one of the most wonderful roles ever written." — James Agee, *Time*

"The film has not the pictorial quality of *Henry V;* it has, however, a rarer virtue, the means in itself to prove that the greatest of Shakespeare's plays can be translated to the screen without loss of dignity to the author and to the immense enjoyment of a public suspicious of his name." — *The Times*

"To some it will be one of the greatest films ever made, to others a deep disappointment. Laurence Olivier leaves no doubt that he is one of our greatest living actors. His rich, moving voice, his expressive face, make of the tortured Dane a figure of deep and sincere tragedy. Arguments about his age and his blond hair cannot detract from the personal triumph of his performance. His liberties with the text, however, are sure to disturb many." — Milton Shulman, *Evening Standard*

"... this is manipulation with a purpose. An immortal play (with its occasionally obscure language, its sliced and separate scenes, acts and intervals) has been turned into an immortal film, telescoped maybe, but continuous and understandable for all of two and a half hours." — Paul Dehn, *Sunday Chronicle*

"Through Olivier, the people's playwright has reached the people. Entertainment thus, for once, has achieved its highest purpose." — Jay Carmody, *The Evening Star*, Washington, D.C.

"Olivier has obviously a cinematic imagination. Yet he has allowed himself to be intoxicated and side-tracked by decor and deep focus and tracking cameras. He has achieved neither first-rate cinema nor first-rate Shakespeare. He could have failed or succeeded more cheaply and more quietly." — Richard Winnington, *News Chronicle*

NOTES

This film sparked off a very lengthy correspondence in *The Times* concerning not so much the cuts as the transpositions and substitution of words; for example, "Hinders" was substituted for "Lets" as being more understandable.

It was during the filming of *Hamlet* that Olivier received both his knighthood and his Oscar for *Henry V*. The latter was presented to him by Ray Milland and Hal Wallis.

Made at a cost of £500,000, in six months, *Hamlet* won four Academy Awards: Best Actor, Best Film, Best Art Director (Carmen Dillon), and Best Set Design (Roger Furse). *Henry V* and *Hamlet* collected Olivier's only Academy Awards.

Notes by Sir Laurence Olivier

I am no writer. One of the dramatic critics — a Scottish one at that — remarked to me the other day, after perusing a so-called essay of mine in some theatre magazine: "If you don't stop trying to write, I warn you I shall try to act Macbeth, and I'll make you come and see it!" I must admit I saw the fellow's point — even though he was a dramatic critic! The cobbler should stick to his last, the player to his part, and the film-director to his film-script.

And yet I suppose it is my bounden duty to proceed once more unto the breach in this matter! I suppose it is expected of me that I should, like a what-d'ye-call-it, unpack my heart with words, and fall a-theorising like a very don, a pedant?

It was — as may well be imagined — with feelings of some trepidation, a kind of fearful awe, that I approached the idea of a *Hamlet* film. Indeed, it will be noticed, and doubtless commented upon, that I took the precaution of being in Australia when the film opened in London! But more seriously, the snares and pitfalls that await anybody who touches so world-famous a masterpiece were only too obvious to me. And, lest there be doubters, or people who question my presumption, I must state that everything done in connection with the film was done on the best obtainable advice. All textual alterations and cuttings were carried out only after close consultation with Alan Dent — that effectual but elusive angel (for I do confess that once or twice at Denham we had occasion to refer to him as "that never-present help in time of trouble"!) In all matters concerned with decor and setting, and all that is euphemistically lumped together as the "art" side of the film, I have been able to call upon Roger Furse — invaluable, responsive and ever-present. The accompanying music has been specially composed by William Walton, and speaks most eloquently for itself. And I cannot let even so bare a list of the due credits pass without a very particular expression of gratitude to Reginald Beck, that nonpareil of cutters, and to my inspired and highly inventive camera-man, Desmond Dickinson. The *Hamlet* film, in short, is the work of a choice little committee, and the most loyal little committee that ever an actor-director has worked for and with.

With Jean Simmons as Ophelia.

Now, I suppose there must be several matters that have to be considered before the very natural fog of controversy that must surround an experiment of this sort can be dispelled. First, *Hamlet* is probably the best known of all the great plays. We are only too well aware of that, and of the certainty that, say what we will, we shall receive dozens of letters, mainly abusive, telling us what we already know, namely, that this or that famous passage has been omitted. Here, the mere fact that the play is so well known helps to put this matter in clearer perspective. For one thing it means that we have had to do all our work, as it were, in the open, because we knew that no careless emendation or sleight-of-hand would pass unnoticed or be tolerated.

It should always be borne in mind when discussing the question of what has been cut, that *Hamlet* is very seldom played in its entirety even on the stage. And it makes a very long evening of over four hours when it is played whole — a running time that is difficult enough in the theatre, and obviously out of the question in the cinema. And it may, too, be noted in passing that we, in this film, have allowed ourselves considerably less licence in the matter of cutting than did that fine English-American actor, Maurice Evans, when he took a version of his superb *Hamlet* to army camps during the war. That *Hamlet* took a stand on the fact that some of the finer shades of the play, that are caught by a select New York audience, would pass over the heads of greater and less instructed masses, who would be bored and demand a swifter action in the plot. We would not, of course, go so far as to say that those who know their *Hamlet* must take into account what has been left out, and that those who do not will never miss it! But think for a moment of the audiences reached by the films who never go to a theatre, and you will appreciate a basic difficulty that determined many of the decisions we made in this matter. And whilst, as I have made clear, we took infinite care and nothing but the best advice, it is possible to be so pernickety in the way of retaining the original that one can follow a process that ends in grieving over the loss of so much Belleforest amongst the encircling Shakespeare (who borrowed the bare bones of his plot from Belleforest!) I hope it may now be appreciated that cuts had to be made. It is much more important to consider what cuts were made, and why. This is not the place to indulge in a recital of the technical difficulties of merging, sequence, montage and other features of film-making, and their difference from production on the stage. But suffice it to say that, allowing for the distinction between the two media, the same basic problems remain, of reducing the length, elucidating the plot, unravelling irrele-

vancies, and relating the result to the type of audience. And although I expect many honest differences of opinion and expressions of regret at the non-inclusion of this or that, I hope it will be admitted that in the main we have tried to make a good, sensible job of it. Bear in mind, all the time, that the cinema is even more insistent on the visual aspect of art than the theatre, that the camera can, and must, nose into corners and magnify details that escape notice or pass muster on the stage. On the screen, too, the essential consideration is for what may be kept in the theatre, on account of their intrinsic interest or beauty respectively, cannot be reconciled with the more closely-knit demands of a two-hour film.

Another bone of contention will undoubtedly be not what we have excluded, but what we have added to the action of the play. The simple fact that I have thought it worthwhile to make a film of *Hamlet*, at the generous instigation of Filippo de Giudice, and that J. Arthur Rank has been prepared to harness his vast and superb organisation to my film, sufficiently indicates what my views are in the matter. Every Shakespeare film must, by its very nature, be a re-creation of a Shakespeare play in a quite different art-medium than that for which it was primarily intended. But does that make it impermissible? If you think it does, you must agree to forbid the performance of Verdi's operas of

Othello and *Falstaff*.

If I did not consider the translation of *Hamlet* to the film to be a legitimate experiment, I would never have attempted it. You may be assured of that. But if that is agreed, it would be folly to expect a film *Hamlet* to resemble in its setting even the best of the theatre productions of *Hamlet* — the *Hamlet*, say, of my dear friend, John Gielgud, at the Haymarket, just as it would be folly to expect the trappings of the Haymarket *Hamlet* to resemble those of the Globe in 1603! It will, I dare say, be objected that the sea-fight should not have been included (there is only a glimpse). But as I see it, it is not to be imagined that the Shakespeare who wrote parts for opposing armies, and tried to turn his little river-side stage into the scenes of Antony's fall and Prospero's island, would not have eagerly welcomed the means to show these places more realistically, if they had been to his hand. Nothing that we know of Shakespeare suggests that he actually enjoyed being "cabin'd, cribb'd, confined" by the rudimentary conditions of the stage for which he wrote.

Of my own interpretation of Hamlet I have nothing to say. I am content to present it on the screen. I have not played the part on the stage since a particularly happy season at the Old Vic nearly eleven years ago. I am deeply sensible of the fact that there have been several distinguished new Hamlets since then, and I can only hope that comparisons will not prove entirely odious for me!

I would take this opportunity, however, of pointing out that this is not the first time that *Hamlet* has been seen on the screen in England. Cecil Hepworth, a pioneer of the cinema, filmed Sir Johnston Forbes-Robertson's performance of *Hamlet*, with his entire company from Drury Lane, in 1913. This was the first, and indeed the last, attempt to translate *Hamlet* into the purely visual medium. It was not meant to be a Shakespeare film — Hepworth had no problems to tackle, such as the non-static camera, that have so concerned us. The film was intended merely as a more or less permanent record of a memorable stage-performance, of something by all accounts — and I say so in all sincerity — the finest *Hamlet* of the present century. Sir Johnston played *Hamlet* first in 1897, at the age of forty-four; he was therefore sixty when he made his entry into the film world! Readers of these notes cannot fail to be interested by this notice of the film, from *The Times* for September 23rd, 1913. It seems to me to have "the tone of the time" about it, the atmosphere of the period. Its brevity, in those days of no paper shortage, when a good half-column was given to the production of any new theatre play, is significant. For the cinema in those

"I must be cruel only to be kind": with Eileen Herlie

days was regarded merely as an amusing new toy!

"September 23rd, 1913. *Hamlet* on the Cinematograph. At the New Gallery Kinema in Regent Street last night a crowded audience saw for the first time a cinematograph film reproducing Sir Johnston Forbes-Robertson's *Hamlet*, as it was presented by his company at Drury Lane. The preservation of this record of the performance has, of course, its value to the large circle of Sir J. Forbes-Robertson's admirers, but few could have failed to feel last night how, in its somewhat audacious effort, the cinematography has exposed its limitations. It was not only that Sir J. Forbes-Robertson's voice had gone, but that no other voice was left to take its place, and that for all the majesty of Shakespeare's verse there were only the cold snippets thrown on the screen to do duty, coupled with an occasional descriptive sentence that might have been better left out.

"But what the cinematograph can do was done to perfection. The pictures were beautifully prepared, and where the play demands action it has been, of course, admirably supplied by the leading members of the company. At the beginning of the play a Marconi message of greeting, sent from the "Mauretania" by Sir J. Forbes-Robertson, was thrown upon the screen. Each member of the audience received a souvenir programme containing a number of illustrations. Two performances of *Hamlet* are to be given daily for a period of four weeks."

It is amusing, by the way, to note, in the light of the subsequent scale of such things, that this film of *Hamlet* cost £10,000 and was "about a mile long"!

So much for films of *Hamlet*, old and new. What of the future? More Shakespeare films . . . ? I hope I shall not set a cat among the critical doves if I say that somewhere at the back of my mind there has long been an increasing insistent picture of a film *Macbeth*, in a blood-bolter'd colour-scheme, with a murky sepia o'er the one half world, and withcraft celebrating pale Hecate's offerings in a glow of bloody red! But that is for the future, and what I have written is sufficient unto the present.

It remains only for me to thank, from the depths of my heart, all those who have helped me and made this enterprise possible. And both I and my wife, who has some holding in these matters, wish to affirm most strongly our faith in the future of British films. To those who fear that we may for a moment have forgotten the stage we say, "Bear with us, filmgoer and playgoer: we love you both!" (From: "Hamlet — the film and the play." World Film Publications, 1948.)

When I was making *Henry V* I had thought about a film of *Hamlet*, but I had not followed up this idea in any detailed way. When the question of a second Shakespearian film came up, however, *Hamlet* seemed the obvious choice. From my experience on *Henry V*, I had learnt that in dealing with *Hamlet*, the only real way to solve the problem of adaptation for the screen was to be ruthlessly bold in adapting the original play.

I find it very difficult to pin down how and when I first conceived the basic idea for the treatment of the film *Hamlet*. Quite suddenly, one day, I visualised the final shot of *Hamlet*. And from this glimpse, I saw how the whole conception of the film could be built up.

I feel it is misleading to couple Shakespeare's play with the film of *Hamlet*, and for this reason. In Shakespeare's play, as in all his plays, there runs a beautifully intricate and complete pattern of character and action. The only satisfactory way of appreciating all that Shakespeare meant by *Hamlet* is to sit down in a theatre and follow a performance of the play in its entirety.

The role of Hamlet has always had a great attraction for actors, partly because it is such a long and impressive one, and partly because it is capable of so many and varied interpretations. In the past, actors have played Hamlet according to a number of ideas, and the play has been so cut as to present these different aspects of Hamlet's character.

In our editing of the play, so that it would make

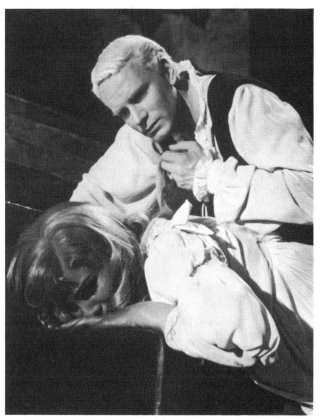

"To a nunnery, go!" Simmons and Olivier.

a film of two and a half hours, instead of a play of four and a half hours, we have worked on the basis of making a new but integral pattern from the original, larger pattern of the play itself. In doing this, we have simplified the story, but inevitably we have lost a good deal.

There are so many jewels in *Hamlet* that it is impossible to make cuts in the play without sacrifice. Amongst other characters who play a continuous part in Shakespeare's *Hamlet*, we have taken out altogether Rosencrantz and Guildenstern, and also Fortinbras. This is a radical approach to adaptation, and because it is so much more than mere condensation, I feel that the film *Hamlet* should be regarded as an *Essay in Hamlet*, and not as a film version of a necessarily abridged classic.

From the beginning, we decided that the sets should be planned as abstractions. This linked up with the idea of a timelessness which I always associated in my mind with *Hamlet*. I say the costumes as a child might, with the King and Queen looking recognisably regal, rather in a conventional, playing-card manner. And the Prince was immemorially clad in the medieval doublet and hose. Ophelia's simplicity was brought out by clothes of almost Victorian innocence.

As for the period of the film *Hamlet*, it is some time, any time, in the remote past.

When we began discussing how to make *Hamlet*,

it was clear that the methods used for *Henry V* were unsuitable for *Hamlet*. In the backgrounds of *Henry V* we had aimed at the effect of missal illustrations. Colour and detail and formally posed figures all combined in making this impression. But in *Hamlet* we wished to achieve the poetic truth ordained by Shakespeare by marrying a sensitive intimacy in the acting to a significant austerity of background.

I determined not to let the beautiful medium of black and white be shuffled out of existence by the popular ascendancy of colour on the screen, until I had explored as thoroughly as possible the beauties and advantages of black and white, so rarely used for a great subject in recent years. One word, "etching", has been used, not entirely correctly I think.

Colour had been essential for *Henry V*. In *Hamlet*, I did at one time examine the notion of filming it in subdued colours — blacks, greys and sepias. But on further consideration, I felt that the final effect would not really have justified the extra problems which use of the technicolor camera always involves. When we came back to our decision to use black and white, it had the added immediate advantage that it could be combined with deep focus photography, whereas we could not have done this had we used colour.

Apart from the obvious advantage, for a film in verse, that deep focus photography enabled us to shoot unusually long scenes, it had the extra merit of lending itself to shots of extreme beauty. I have in mind in particular one shot nicknamed, "The longest distance love-scene on record".

In this scene, Hamlet is sitting in a chair, and through a long series of arches, he sees Ophelia coming towards him. Unknown to Hamlet, she has been warned by her brother, and particularly by her father, to avoid the Prince, and this time, Polonius is hiding behind a pillar. He is invisible to Hamlet, but Ophelia can see him, and when he beckons her away, she turns aside. But to Hamlet, and to the audience who see her from behind Hamlet's shoulders, it looks as though Ophelia has avoided him of her own free will. With the use of deep focus photography, every line of her figure is beautifully distinct as she walks slowly down the long corridors.

In some cases, an actor is over 150 feet away from the camera, yet with deep focus he is seen by the audience with perfect clearness.

We have purposely planned the film with spacious, empty sets. No piece of furniture appears on the screen unless it plays a necessary part in the film, either when it is first seen, or later on in the story. In this way, each piece, whether table, chair or bed, becomes an object of increased significance, and makes its own tiny contribution to the general pattern of the film.

In film work, my preference is for the job of director. I would have liked to have found an actor of sufficient standing to carry the role on whom I could have impressed my interpretation of the character of Hamlet without the actor resenting it. For myself, I feel that my style of acting is more suited to stronger character roles, such as Hotspur and Henry V, rather than to the lyrical, poetical role of Hamlet.

In the end, I thought it simpler to play Hamlet myself, but one reason why I dyed my hair was so as to avoid the possibility of Hamlet later being identified with me. I wanted audiences seeing the film to say, not, "There is Laurence Olivier dressed like Hamlet", but "That is Hamlet".

In the production of the film, I would first of all rehearse the actors in the appropriate scenes. If Hamlet were included, then I used an 'understudy' for grouping and so on. Then I would rehearse myself, and with Reginald Beck and Anthony Bushell standing by, with advice and suggestions, the scenes would be shot.

When work on the floor was finished, the film moved to another stage, in the cutting rooms, where Reginald Beck, that erstwhile best of all cutters, and I, still supervised it. It is a mistake to think that a film is virtually finished when the actors go home. A great deal of rarely publicised work goes on, concerned with editing the film, adding sound and visual effects, fitting in the music to the appropriate sequences, and generally arriving at the final copy of the film.

In our script of *Hamlet*, I believe — and I hope — that we have made the story easy to follow for people who are deterred by Shakespeare himself. The actual story of *Hamlet* is both fascinating and alive. It cuts cleanly away from the older-fashioned concept of heroism and villainy, where characters are irrevocably black or white.

Hamlet, the greatest of all plays, which has kept commentators enthralled for four centuries, was the first to be created by an author with the courage to give his audience a hero with none of the usual excursions of heroism. Perhaps he was the first pacifist, perhaps Dr. Jones is sound in his diagnosis of the Oedipus complex, perhaps there is justification in the many other complexes that have been foisted on to him — perhaps he just thought too much, that is, if a man *can* think too much . . . I prefer to think of him as a nearly great man — damned by lack of resolution, as all but one in a hundred are.

(From "The Film *Hamlet*." Saturn Press, 1948.)

107

THE MAGIC BOX

1951

Festival Films Productions. British Lion Corp. *Country:* G.B. *Running time:* 118 minutes. *Producer:* Ronald Neame. *Director:* John Boulting. *Screenplay:* Eric Ambler. *Production manager:* Bob McNaughton. *Continuity:* June Faithfull. *Photography:* Jack Cardiff. *Camera operator:* Arthur Ibbetson. *Production designer:* John Bryan. *Assistant art director:* T. Hopewell-Ash. *Set dresser:* Dario Simoni. *Editor:* Richard Best. *Costume designer:* Julia Squire.

CAST

Renee Asherson. . . . . *Miss Tagg*
Richard Attenborough . . . . *Jack Carter*
Robert Beatty . . . . *Lord Beaverbrook*
Martin Boddey . . . . *Sitter in Bath Studio*
Edward Chapman . . . . *Father in Family Group*
John Charlesworth . . . . *Graham Friese-Greene*
Maurice Colbourne . . . . . *Bride's father at wedding*
Roland Culver . . . . *First company promoter*
John Howard Davies . . . . . . *Maurice Friese-Greene*
Michael Denison . . . . . . *Connaught rooms reporter*
Robert Donat . . . . *William Friese-Greene*
Joan Dowling . . . . *Friese-Greene maid*
Henry Edwards . . . . *Butler at Fox Talbot's*
Mary Ellis . . . . *Mrs. Collings*
Marjorie Fielding. . . . . *Elderly Viscountess*
Robert Flemyng . . . . *Doctor in surgery*
Leo Genn . . . . *Maida Vale doctor*
Marius Goring . . . . *House Agent*
Everly Gregg . . . . *Bridegroom's mother at wedding*
Joyce Grenfell. *Mrs. Clare*
Robertson Hare. . . . . *Sitter in Bath Studio*
Kathleen Harrison . . . . *Mother in family group*
William Hartnell . . . . *Recruiting sergeant*
Joan Hickson. . . . . *Mrs. Stukely*
Thora Hird . . . . *Doctor's housekeeper*
Stanley Holloway . . . . *Broker's man*
Patrick Holt. . . . . *Sitter in Bath Studio*
Michael Hordern . . . . *Official receiver*
Jack Hulbert . . . . *1st Holborn policeman*
Sidney James. . . . . *Sergeant in storeroom*
Glynis Johns . . . . *May Jones*
Mervyn Johns . . . . *Pawnbroker*
Margaret Johnston. . . . . *Edith Friese-Greene*
Barry Jones. . . . . *Bath Doctor*
Peter Jones . . . . . *Industry man, Connaught rooms*
James Kenney . . . . *Kenneth Friese-Greene*

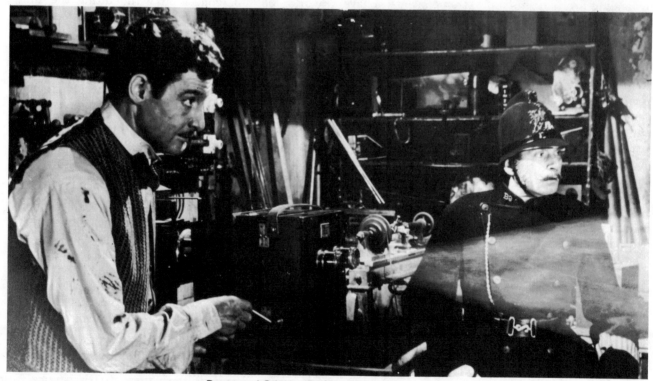

Donat and Olivier, "Milking the big moment".

Ann Lancaster......*Bridesmaid in wedding group*
Herbert Lomas...........*Warehouse manager*
John Longdon......*Speaker in Connaught rooms*
Bessie Love......*Bride's mother, wedding group*
Miles Malleson............*Orchestra conductor*
Garry Marsh........*Second Company promoter*
Muir Matheson.............*Sir Arthur Sullivan*
A. E. Matthews...*Old gentleman, Bond St. Studio*
John McCallum..........*Sitter in Bath Studio*
Bernard Miles................*Cousin Alfred*
Richard Murdoch.........*Sitter in Bath Studio*
David Oake.............*Claude Friese-Greene*
Laurence Olivier........*2nd Holborn policeman*
Cecil Parker......*1st platform man at Connaught*
Frank Pettingell...*Bridegroom's father at wedding*
Norman Pierce......*Speaker in Connaught rooms*
Eric Portman.................*Arthur Collings*
Dennis Price.......*Assistant in Bond St. Studio*
Michael Redgrave....*Mr. Lege, instrument maker*
Peter Reynolds.....*Bridegroom, wedding group*
Margaret Rutherford...............*Lady Pond*
Maria Schell..............*Helena Friese-Greene*
Janette Scott..............*Ethel Friese-Greene*
Ronald Shiner............*Fairground barker*
Sheila Sim.....................*Nursemaid*
Madame Slobodskaya....*Soloist at Bath Concert*
John Stuart.....*2nd platform man at Connaught*
Marianne Stone........*Bride in wedding group*
Basil Sydney..............*William Fox Talbot*
Ernest Thesiger..........*Earl, Bond St. Studio*
David Tomlinson........*Assistant in laboratory*
Sybil Thorndike.........*Sitter in Bath Studio*
Cecil Trouncer...................*John Rudge*
Michael Trubshawe.......*Sitter in Bath Studio*
Peter Ustinov...................*Industry man*
Charles Victor...*Industry man, Connaught rooms*
Kay Walsh.................*Hotel receptionist*
Norman Watson......*Doctor in Connaught rooms*
Emlyn Williams...............*Bank manager*
Harcourt Williams..*Tom, workman at Lege & Co.*
Googie Withers...........*Sitter in Bath Studio*
Joan Young..............*Glove shop 'dragon'*

STORY
The story of William Friese-Greene's struggles, first as a young Bristol photographer and then as an inventor, trying to raise money to work on his idea of a motion-picture camera. Laurence Olivier plays a policeman who is called in off the street to witness Friese-Greene's first success. An all-star showcase for Festival of Britain year.

CRITICS' CIRCLE
"Sir Laurence Olivier appears as a bewildered city policeman, dragged off his beat by the inventor in the middle of the night, to form an audience for

Waylaying of a "Stolid, bewildered London bobby".

one of the first public performances of moving pictures. This scene is brilliant in its economy and incisiveness, and in the subdued eloquence of its pantomime. It is also unselfish, with one of the greatest actors of our time deliberately serving as a 'feed' in the interests of the story."—C. A. Lejeune, *Britain Today*

"Best sequence: Friese-Greene excitedly demonstrating his newly-perfected magic box by projecting flickering Hyde Park scenes in his laboratory in the dead of night to an audience of one: a stolid, bewildered London bobby, pungently portrayed by Laurence Olivier." — *Time*

"There is a very fine scene in which a stolid and puzzled policeman (Laurence Olivier) is called in by the excited inventor to see his first moving picture." — Harold Hobson, *Christian Science Monitor*

"The policeman is played by a be-whiskered Laurence Olivier and he and Donat milk the big moment of more tenseness and eye-moistening emotion than you would have thought possible." — Leonard Mosley, *Daily Express*

NOTES
The Magic Box was the British Film Industry's principal contribution to the Festival of Britain. The National Film Finance Corporation lost nearly all its money due to the box-office failure of this (generally felt) worthy, though uninspired, film.

CARRIE

1952

Paramount. *Country:* U.S.A. *Running time:* 118 minutes. *Producer and director:* William Wyler. *Associate producer:* Lester Koenig. *Screenplay:* Ruth and Augustus Goetz, *based on* Theodore Dreiser's *novel "Sister Carrie".* *Photography:* Victor Milne. *Editor:* Robert Swink. *Art directors:* Hale Pereira and Roland Anderson.

CAST

Laurence Olivier . . . . *George Hurstwood*
Jennifer Jones . . . . *Carrie Meeber*
Miriam Hopkins . . . . *Julia Hurstwood*
Eddie Albert . . . . *Charles Drouet*
Basil Ruysdael . . . . *Mr. Fitzgerald*
Ray Teal . . . . *Allan*
Barry Kelleg . . . . *Slawson*
Sara Berner . . . . *Mrs. Oransky*
William Reynolds . . . . *George Hurstwood Jr.*
Mary Murphy . . . . *Jessica Hurstwood*
Harry Hayden . . . . *O'Brien*
Charles Halton . . . . *Factory foreman*
Walter Baldwin . . . . *Carrie's father*
Dorothy Adams . . . . *Carrie's mother*
Jacqueline Dewit . . . . *Carrie's sister*
Harlan Briggs . . . . *Joe Brant*
Donald Kerr . . . . *Slawson's bartender*
Lester Sharpe . . . . *Mr. Blum*
Don Beddoe . . . . *Mr. Goodman*
John Alvin . . . . *Stage manager*

STORY

Carrie leaves a small midwestern town for Chicago. On the train she meets Charlie Drouet, a self-assured salesman. When she is unable to find work in Chicago, Carrie goes to Drouet and becomes his mistress. There is talk of marriage but Carrie meets George Hurstwood, a restaurant manager who falls in love with her and steals $10,000, then leaves his family and goes to New York with Carrie. The embezzlement is discovered and he returns the money, leaving them both in total poverty. Hurstwood is unable to find work and Carrie leaves him for a stage career. Hurstwood degenerates totally.

With Jennifer Jones

CRITICS' CIRCLE

". . . with a light American accent, Olivier plays with slumbrous fire which never becomes sleepy. And he looks almost too elegant." — John Barber, *Daily Express*

"Wyler has delicately caught the tragedy of a man's downfall and decay; and Sir Laurence Olivier's acting is a triumph of autumnal sensibility." — Dilys Powell, *Sunday Times*

". . . only Sir Laurence fights through the layers of melancholy to emerge as recognisably human." — Philip Day, *Sunday Times*

"The eminent British actor was thought too elegant and alien for the role of Mr. Dreiser's middle-aged hero who went to ruin out of love for a pretty girl.

With Jennifer Jones: "a triumph of autumnal sensibility".

As it turned out, however, Mr. Olivier gives the film its closest contact with the book." — Bosley Crowther, *New York Times*

"The best acting of his career." — Richard Winnington, *News Chronicle*

NOTES

Olivier, in search of a Hollywood job while Vivien Leigh was making *A Streetcar Named Desire*, agreed to make *Carrie*. Cary Grant had already turned down the part of George Hurstwood in the film. Laurence Olivier spent a good deal of time learning American speech patterns and did his best to stay away from the press while in Hollywood. He finally agreed to a press conference on the condition that arch-columnist Sheilah Graham did not attend.

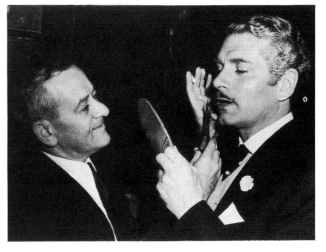

On the *Carrie* set.

THE BEGGAR'S OPERA

1953

Imperadio Pictures Ltd. *Distributed by:* British Lion Films. *Country:* G.B. Technicolor. *Running time:* 94 minutes. *Producers:* Laurence Olivier and Herbert Wilcox. *Director:* Peter Brook. *Screenplay:* Denis Cannan, *adapted from the comic operetta by* John Gay. *Additional dialogue and lyrics:* Christopher Fry. *Music arranged and composed by:* Sir Arthur Bliss. *Technicolor consultant:* John Bridge. *Photography:* Guy Green. *Art director:* William C. Andrews. *Opera sets and costumes:* George Wakhevitch. *Supervising editor:* Reginald Beck. *Production manager:* J. D. Wilcox. *Associate producer:* Eric Goodhead. *Sound recordists:* Peter Handford and Red Law. *Assistant director:* Frank Hollands. *Production assistant:* John Braybourne. *Special effects:* Wally Veevers and George Samuels. *Wardrobe supervisor:* Maude Churchill. *Set dresser:* Leonard Townsend. *Repetiteur:* William Blezard. *Score conducted by:* Muir Mathieson.

CAST

Laurence Olivier	*Captain Macheath*
Stanley Holloway	*Lockit*
George Devine	*Peachum*
Mary Clare	*Mrs. Peachum*
Athene Seyler	*Mrs. Trapes*
Dorothy Tutin	*Polly Peachum*
Daphne Anderson	*Lucy Lockit*
Hugh Griffith	*The Beggar*
Margot Grahame	*The Actress*
Dennis Cannan	*The Footman*
George Rose	*1st Turnkey*
Stuart Burge	*1st Prisoner*
Cyril Conway	*2nd Prisoner*
Gerald Lawson	*3rd Prisoner*
Eileen Harvey	*Young Female Traveller*
Edward Pryor	*Filch*
Eric Pohlmann	*Innkeeper*
Edith Coates	*Mrs. Coaxer*
Yvonne Furneaux	*Jenny Diver*
Kenneth Williams	*Jack, the pot boy*
Sandra Dorne	*Sukey Tawdrey*
Laurence Naismith	*Matt of the Mint*
Max Brent	*A Drunkard*
Mercy Haystead	*Dolly Trall*
Patricia Raine	*Mrs Slammekin*
Jocelyn James	*Molly Brazen*
Isabel George	*Mrs. Vixen*
Helen Christie	*Betty Doxey*
John Kidd	*2nd turnkey*
H. C. Walton	*3rd turnkey*
Eugene Leahy	*4th turnkey*
Edgar Norfolk	*5th turnkey*
Oliver Hunter	*1st Chairman*
John Baker	*2nd Chairman*
Madge Brindley	*Gin seller*
Felix Felton	*The governor*
Tamba Alleney	*Negro Page*
Terence Greenidge	*Chaplain*
Billy Wells	*Hangman*

STORY

This film uses the play-within-a-play device and is set in London in 1741 among the beggars and thieves of Gay's original opera. Highwayman Macheath is betrayed by his wife's parents and he is imprisoned. His two mistresses meet at the jail.

With the Beggar (Hugh Griffith) in Newgate prison.

Lucy steals the keys and releases him but he is recaptured at the gaming house and led to the gallows. He is reprieved at the last moment.

CRITICS' CIRCLE

"Olivier himself plays the dashing Macheath with keen appreciation of the satire implicit in the role. He also sings his own part, revealing a light tenor that is always agreeable if not always true . . . Opera on film requires a bold hand as well. Sir Laurence has played it to perfection." — Arthur Knight, *Saturday Review*

"Olivier has steadfastly preserved, even cherished the integrity of the originals. But this veteran of theatre and film is perceptive of the differences between the two media. His Shakespearian films achieved a remarkably successful compromise in a field where compromise is generally disastrous." — Arthur Knight, *op cit*

"Once or twice Sir Laurence uses his eyes . . . and reminds us what a wonderful display of rakish sex-appeal and gallantry we were expecting from his Captain Macheath; alas, here a dull and curiously sombre hero." — Philip Hope-Wallace, *Manchester Guardian*

"Olivier's Macheath, to my mind, is the most comfortable piece of work he has given us yet in pictures. He romps through the part, whether acting, singing, dancing or riding, without any touch of self-consciousness, and as though all these exercises were a joy; and the player's impression of ease, of relaxation, is irresistably communicated to the audience." — C. A. Lejeune, *The Observer*

NOTES

This was Peter Brook's first professional film, and it was beset by troubles. Olivier injured a calf muscle in one of the duels, setting the schedule back by nearly a month. In all it cost a quarter of a million pounds, which Korda recovered from Jack Warner in America. But for Olivier professionally, and for Wilcox commercially, *The Beggar's Opera* was a considerable failure. A last minute title-change to *Macheath The Highwayman* was rejected by Olivier.

A QUEEN IS CROWNED

1953

J. Arthur Rank. *Country:* G.B. Technicolor. *Running time:* 90 minutes. *Producer:* Castleton Knight. *Narration:* Sir Laurence Olivier. *Written by:* Christopher Fry. *Musical advisor:* Sir Malcolm Sargent. *Special music by:* Guy Warrach. *Played by:* The London Symphony Orchestra.

This was a documentary made at the Coronation of Queen Elizabeth II. It includes the coronation procession and the service in Westminster Abbey.

CRITICS' CIRCLE
"Christopher Fry's commentary, intensely spoken by Sir Laurence Olivier, struck me as being too overawed for the occasion. It never descended to the natural." — Milton Shulman, *Evening Standard*

". . . with an eloquent commentary by Christopher Fry finely spoken by Sir Laurence Olivier, *A Queen Is Crowned* is the richest and most stirring film I have ever seen." — Campbell Dixon, *Daily Telegraph*

NOTES
A Queen Is Crowned was voted by the International Press the best documentary of 1953.

With Christopher Fry and Castleton Knight preparing the commentary.

RICHARD III

1955

Laurence Olivier Productions — London Films — Big Ben Films. *Country:* G.B. Technicolor. Vista-Vision. *Running time:* 158 minutes. *Producer and director:* Laurence Olivier. *Associate director:* Anthony Bushell. *Production designer:* Roger Furse. *Art director:* Carmen Dillon. *Photography:* Otto Heller. *Production supervisor:* John Gossage. *Editor:* Helga Cranston. *Camera operator:* Denys Coop. *Special effects:* Wally Veevers. *Text adviser:* Alan Dent. *Production manager:* Jack Martin. *Assistant director:* Gerry O'Hara. *Continuity:* Pamela Davies. *Sound supervisor:* John Cox. *Sound recordists:* George Stephenson and Red Law. *Assistant art director:* Arthur Lawson. *Sound editor:* Bert Rule. *Chief make-up artist:* Tony Sforzini. *Hairdresser:* Gladys Atkinson. *Title designs and set dressings:* Roger Ramsdell. *Scenic artist:* Robert White. *Masters of the horse:* Jeremy Taylor and Jack Curran. *Sword play:* Bernard Hepton and John Greenwood. *Music:* Sir William Walton. *Played by:* The Royal Philharmonic Orchestra. *Conducted by:* Muir Mathieson.

With Claire Bloom as the Lady Anne.

CAST

Cedric Hardwicke	*Edward IV*
Nicholas Hannen	*Archbishop of Canterbury*
Laurence Olivier	*Richard III*
Ralph Richardson	*Buckingham*
John Gielgud	*Clarence*
Mary Kerridge	*Queen Elizabeth*
Pamela Brown	*Jane Shore*
Paul Huson	*Prince of Wales*
Stewart Allen	*Page to Richard*
Claire Bloom	*Lady Anne*
Russell Thorndike	*1st Priest*
Wally Pascoe and Norman Fisher	*Two Monks*
Andrew Cruickshank	*Brackenbury*
Clive Morton	*Rivers*
Terrence Greenidge	*Scrivenor*
Norman Wooland	*Catesby*
Alec Clunes	*Hastings*
Dan Cunningham	*Grey*
Douglas Wilmer	*Dorset*
Laurence Naismith	*Stanley*
Michael Gough	*1st murderer*
Michael Ripper	*2nd murderer*
Helen Haye	*Duchess of York*
Andy Shine	*Young Duke of York*
Roy Russell	*Abbot*
George Woodbridge	*Lord Mayor of London*
Esmond Knight	*Ratcliffe*
John Laurie	*Lovel*
Peter Williams	*Messenger to Hastings*
Timothy Bateson	*Ostler*
Willoughby Gray	*2nd Priest*
Anne Wilton	*Scrubwoman*
Bill Shine	*Beadle*
Derek Prentice and Deering Wells	*Two clergymen*
Richard Bennett	*George Stanley*
Patrick Troughton	*Tyrell*
Brian Nissen, Alexander Davion, Lane Meddick and Robert Bishop	*Messengers to Richard*
John Phillips	*Norfolk*
Stanley Baker	*Richmond*

STORY

Shakespeare's version of the murderous and cunning rise of Richard Gloucester to the throne of England and his eventual defeat and death on Bosworth Field

Olivier with (l to r) George Woodbridge, Nicholas Hannen, Paul Huson and Ralph Richardson.

at the hands of Henry Tudor, Earl of Richmond.

CRITICS' CIRCLE

"A feast for Shakespeare fans, but not my cup of tea." — *Daily Mirror*

"Wherever the play was loose-jointed or ill-fitting, Sir Laurence has been its tinker and its tailor — but never once (as so often happens with other films) its butcher. ... Sir Laurence's own performance as Richard is dazzling." — Paul Dehn, *News Chronicle*

"Sir Laurence's stage Richard III was by general consent the most exciting within memory. His screen version ... should have a comparable success with a much wider public." — Campbell Dixon, *Daily Telegraph*

"It embalms in celluloid one of the greatest Shake-

spearian performances of our day. Olivier plays his Richard for laughs. And he raises the grisly humour of the horror comic to the level of genius." — Alan Brien, *Evening Standard*

"(This film) is a huge, stirring, splendid, sardonic version of Shakespeare's historical melodrama. To fear disappointment with Olivier's stage Richard in mind is unnecessary ... perhaps something is gained by the intimacy which cinema permits." — Dilys Powell, *Sunday Times*

"Somehow this *Richard III* never, with pennants streaming and trumpets sounding, storms to decisive victory." — *The Times*

"Laurence Olivier interprets the title rôle with a mastery so complete that Richard III in this generation can surely never be himself again." — *Time*

The strange wooing of the Lady Anne

Richard displays his withered hand to Buckingham

"A more exciting *Richard III* than anything that the stage has ever done or is ever likely to do." — Milton Shulman, *Sunday Express*

NOTES

Although this version of *Richard III*, made by Olivier under the aegis of Alexander Korda, begins with a passage from *Henry VI Part III*, Lady Anne follows the wrong body, her wooing is split in two, fragments from Colley Cibber are introduced and it completely cuts out Queen Margaret, it was nevertheless considered, in spirit, absolutely right and greeted by critics with such words as "magnificent" and "dazzling".

In an unprecedented deal the National Broadcasting Corporation of the U.S.A. bought the television rights to *Richard III* for $500,000. It was shown on American television on the third of December, 1956 in the afternoon with three General Motors commercial breaks, and premiered in the cinema that night. Although it was transmitted in colour (complete with ads for a car battery "More powerful than all the horses in *Richard III*") there were still few colour sets then.

It did not make money in the States and because of its failure to get good box-office takings Olivier could not, after Korda's death, raise the money for the film of *Macbeth* which he wanted to make. However on its re-release in 1966 *Variety* reported "*Richard III* breaking house records".

Richard III won three British Film Academy Awards for 1955: Best performance by a British actor; Best British film; Best film from any source.

It won the Silver Bear (2nd prize) at the Berlin Festival 1956.

Laurence Olivier was again nominated as Best Actor for the Academy Awards, 1956. Yul Brynner won the Oscar for *The King and I*.

"A Horse! A Horse! My Kingdom for a Horse!" (with Norman Wooland as Catesby).

THE PRINCE AND THE SHOWGIRL

1957

A Warner Bros. presentation of a film by Marilyn Monroe Productions Inc. and L.O.P. Ltd. *Country:* G.B. Technicolor. *Running time:* 115 minutes. *Producer and director:* Laurence Olivier. *Executive producer:* Milton H. Greene. *Screenplay:* Terence Rattigan, *based on a play The Sleeping Prince by:* Terence Rattigan. *Photography:* Jack Cardiff. *Music:* Richard Addinsell. *Conducted by:* Muir Mathieson. *Dances arranged by:* William Chappell. *Editor:* Jack Harris.

CAST

Marilyn Monroe	*Elsie Marina*
Laurence Olivier	*Charles, Prince Regent*
Sybil Thorndike	*Queen Dowager*
Richard Wattis	*Northbrooke*
Jeremy Spenser	*King Nicholas*
Esmond Knight	*Hoffman*
Paul Hardwick	*Major Domo*
Rosamund Greenwood	*Maud*
Aubrey Dexter	*The Ambassador*
Maxine Audley	*Lady Sunningdale*
Harold Greenwood	*Call Boy*
Andreas Melandrinos	*Valet with violin*
Jean Kent	*Springfield*
Daphne Anderson	*Fanny*
Gillian Owen	*Maggie*
Vera Day	*Betty*
Margot Lister	*Lottie*
Charles Victor	*Theatre Manager*
David Horne	*The foreign officer*
Dennis Edwards	*Head Valet*
Gladys Henson	*Dresser*

STORY

Grand Duke Charles, Prince Regent of Carpathia, visits London in 1911 for the Coronation of George V. With him are his young son King Nicholas and his mother-in-law, the Queen Dowager. The Prince Regent meets an American showgirl, Elsie Marina, and invites her to supper at the Embassy where he makes unsuccessful passes. After drinking too much she falls asleep. In the morning she realises she has fallen in love but it is not reciprocal. The Prince Regent is annoyed at her tenacity which is encouraged, somewhat vaguely, by the Queen Dowager. Nicholas, annoyed at being treated by his father as a child, plots a coup with the Germans. Elsie discovers this and mediates between father and son, and finally wins the Prince Regent who must return to Carpathia to rule for 18 months before handing over the government to Nicholas. They promise to meet again after that time.

Olivier and Monroe "Stooping to conquer"

CRITICS' CIRCLE

"... great fun if you don't take it seriously. Certainly its author doesn't. Terence Rattigan is just playing a game, amusing us for two hours, and the actors enjoy the charade immensely. They try to look earnest but a twinkle in the eye betrays them. In the case of Olivier, the twinkle must fight its way through a thick monocle to reach the outside world and it does. This is a performance of rich, subtle humour." — William K. Zinsser, *New York Herald Tribune*

"Instead of concentrating on making a good film, too much of his (Olivier's) energy has gone into perfecting a grotesque characterization for himself." — Peter Tudor, *Sunday Express*

"... not one of Sir Laurence's best films. His work should be successful but he stoops to conquer. As producer-director he occasionally allows himself, as

Rattigan's odd couple.

Directing *The Prince and the Showgirl.*

Sir Laurence and Dame Sybil.

an actor, a moment of perfection — the ghost hint of a smile in the coronation carriage, the snip-second punctuation of the line in which he gives his age as 'forty'." — C. A. Lejeune, *The Observer*

"What gives *The Prince and the Showgirl* its special delight is the stylised work of its co-stars, Marilyn Monroe and Laurence Olivier, and the wit and grace of Olivier's direction." — Arthur Knight, *Saturday Review*

NOTES
This film was stormy in production with lower-echelon studio observers selling 'the true story' to the popular press of the time. In Rattigan's original stage play, Vivien Leigh had played the Monroe part opposite her then husband; a decade later, the play resurfaced in America as a Noël Coward musical called *The Girl Who Came to Supper.* But Olivier still preferred the play's original title *The Sleeping Prince.* The film title (wished on him by American backers) sounded, he said, like "an old Betty Grable musical".

En route to the Coronation: Olivier and Monroe, Sybil Thorndike and Richard Wattis.

THE DEVIL'S DISCIPLE

1959

Hecht-Hill-Lancaster Films and Brynaprod S.A. *Distributed by:* United Artists. *Country:* G.B. *Running time:* 82 minutes. *Producer:* Harold Hecht. *Director:* Guy Hamilton. *Screenplay:* John Dighton and Ronald Kibbee, *based on the play by:* George Bernard Shaw. *Photography:* Jack Hildyard. *Editor:* Alan Osbiston. *Art direction:* Terrence Verity and Edward Carrere. *Musical score:* Richard Rodney Bennett.

CAST

Burt Lancaster. . . . . *Anthony Anderson*
Kirk Douglas . . . . *Richard Dudgeon*
Laurence Olivier . . . . *General Burgoyne*
Janette Scott. . . . .*Judith Anderson*
Eva LeGallienne . . . . *Mrs. Dudgeon*
Harry Andrews . . . . *Major Swindon*
Basil Sydney . . . .*Lawyer Hawkins*
George Rose . . . . *British Sergeant*
Neil McCallum. . . . . *Christopher Dudgeon*
Mervyn Jones . . . .*Rev. Maindeck Parshotter*
David Horne . . . . *William*
Erik Chitty . . . .*Titus*
Jennie Jones . . . .*Essie*

STORY

During the American War of Independence a small New England town is taken over by the British General Burgoyne and his men after their march down from Canada. To subdue the rebellious colonists, the British hang a prominent citizen, Timothy Dudgeon. The village pastor, Anthony Anderson, arrives home to find his wife comforting the widow. Soon after, the hanged man's son, Richard, descends to cause trouble and spur on the revolution. The pastor admires young Dudgeon but worries that his wife does too. Burgoyne, who would rather be in London than dealing with rebellious colonials, is talked into hanging another villager as an example. The army decides on the pastor but mistakenly arrests Dudgeon when he is found at the Anderson home. Dudgeon allows himself to be arrested and tried, partly for a whim and partly to help Anderson who has joined the Revolutionary forces. Anderson intercepts an important message and uses it against Burgoyne to save Dudgeon an instant before the noose is put around his neck. The pastor gets his wife back and Dudgeon goes to tea with the General who (the voice at the end tells us) surrendered at Saratoga only three weeks later.

CRITICS' CIRCLE

"The greatest actor in the world. . . Olivier gives the performance of his life, making Lancaster and

With Janette Scott and Kirk Douglas.

Off set with Janette Scott, Kirk Douglas and Burt Lancaster

Douglas look like stupid oafs who have wandered back from a western." — *Evening Standard*, front-page review

"... (Olivier's) appearances are as water in, if not a desert, at least a dryish and unsatisfactory place. Sir Laurence's specialty here is civilised irony and beautifully civilised and ironic he is — but then he is allowed some of Shaw's own lines to speak." — *The Times*

"Olivier as Burgoyne, is in enormously good humour, delivers his speeches with a rare bite and is exactly what Shaw might have asked for, if he had been available to deliver advice on casting and filming." — Hollis Alpert, *Saturday Review*

"Laurence Olivier, as always a master of irony, gives a study of the utmost polish and perception." — Patrick Gibbs, *Daily Telegraph*

"And though, as the English General Burgoyne, Olivier loses the American War of Independence, he wins the fight for screen supremacy (over Douglas and Lancaster) while barely stretching his talents to a tenth of their capacity." — Margaret Hinxman, *Daily Herald*

"Burgoyne: "History, Sir, will tell lies as usual."

THE ENTERTAINER

1960

Bryanston presents a Woodfall Production. *Distributed by:* British Lion Films in association with Bryanston Films. *Country:* G.B. *Running time:* 104 minutes (on release 96 minutes). *Producer:* Harry Saltzman. *Director:* Tony Richardson. *Associate producer:* John Croydon. *Screenplay:* John Osborne and Nigel Kneale, *adapted from the play by:* John Osborne. *Photography:* Oswald Morris. *Music composed and conducted by:* John Addison. *Associate music director:* Ronnie Cass. *Art director:* Ralph Brinton. *Production manager:* R. L. M. Davidson. *Editor:* Alan Osbiston. *Assistant director:* Peter Yates. *Camera operator:* Denys Coop. *Assistant art director:* Ted Marshall. *Continuity:* Margaret Shipway. *Sound editor:* Chris Greenham. *Make-up:* Tony Sforzini. *Hairdresser:* Bill Griffiths. *Wardrobe:* Barbara Gillette. *Sound:* Peter Handford and Bob Jones. *Laurence Olivier's numbers staged by:* Honor Blair.

CAST

Laurence Olivier	*Archie Rice*
Brenda de Banzie	*Phoebe Rice*
Joan Plowright	*Jean*
Roger Livesey	*Billy*
Alan Bates	*Frank*
Daniel Massey	*Graham*
Albert Finney	*Mick Rice*
Miriam Karlin	*Soubrette*
Shirley Anne Field	*Tina*
Thora Hird	*Mrs Lapford*
Tony Longridge	*Mr. Lapford*
Mcdonald Hobley	*Film star*
Charles Gray	*Columnist*
Angie & Debbie Dean	*Sisters (Alhambra)*
Geoffrey Toone	*Hubbard*
James Culliford	*Cobber Carson*
Gilbert Davis	*Brother Bill*
Anthony Oliver	*Interviewer*
Jo Linden	*Gloria*
Mercia Turner	*Britannia*
Vicky Travers	*Other Nude*
Beryl & Bobo	*Trampoline Act*
Herman & Constance Welles	*Scots singers*
The Clippers (Ken Thompson)	*Rock 'n' Roll Trio*

With Joan Plowright, Alan Bates and Brenda de Banzie

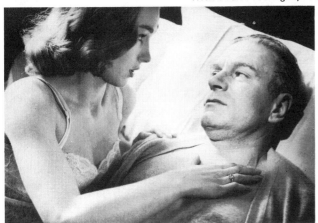
With Shirley Anne Field.

With Joan Plowright.

STORY

Archie Rice is an old-time vaudeville performer, sinking into final defeat. His daughter returns to the family from a devastating experience in London but finds no solace in Morecambe where Archie is starring in a summer show, and Phoebe Rice is seeking refuge in gin. Archie, despite schemes to stay in showbusiness, has to admit defeat after his father, Billy, a once famous entertainer, dies in the wings. The backers close Archie's show and Osborne's metaphor for a crumbling Britain is complete.

CRITICS' CIRCLE

"The result is something like a spotty opera in which there are some good scenes but not much overall validity... Laurence Olivier, in the title role, does the best impersonation of a song and dance man by an actor since Alfred Lunt in *Idiot's Delight*; but otherwise his performance is, for Olivier, somewhat disappointing. He creates a telling self-disgust (the picnic scene with the daughter is particularly good) but he indulges in Hamlet-y gazes too deep for Archie (the scene in the caravan) and sometimes offers us lip-chewing *vice* acting. The net result is a gallery of studied effects, some of which succeed resoundingly, rather than a seamless, realised performance." — Stanley Kauffman, *The New Republic*

"There may be strains and lapses in the film and Sir Laurence may sometimes break the firm lines of Mr. Osborne's dialogue with a rocketing, fantastic and unforgettable display of broken and contrasting hopes, wishes, despairs, desires and resolutions, yet *The Entertainer*, with its Capital letters, is a work of art and the entertainer himself, humbly bereft of them, a man of courage." — *The Times*

With Shirley Anne Field on *The Entertainer* set.

"Olivier's performance is still impressive — though not quite as sharp as it seemed on stage where it spiritually belongs." — Fred Majdalany, *Daily Mail*

"He is the pearl in this very bad oyster . . . Olivier filled this husk with flesh and blood and created a figure of tragedy." — Leonard Mosley, *Daily Express*

"Laurence Olivier, a Roman patrician in *Spartacus*, here re-creates the role he played in John Osborne's play of a couple of years ago and a flawless piece of acting it is." — Brendan Gill, *The New Yorker*

". . . Sir Laurence Olivier gives his celebrated performance as a fifth-rate music-hall comic. A justly celebrated performance it is too, though it remains, to my mind, the poorest and least interesting thing which the Western world's most magical actor has ever perpetrated." — Derek Monsey, *Sunday Express*

NOTES
Generally, the critics were evenly divided on this film — they either loved it or hated it, but few gave it the careful critical attention which had been awarded to Olivier's performance in Osborne's original stage play.

There was a good deal of fuss over the censor's certificate for *The Entertainer*. In the end it became Olivier's first X film.

Laurence Olivier was again nominated for an Academy Award as Best Actor, 1960. It was won by Burt Lancaster for *Elmer Gantry*.

THE POWER AND THE GLORY

1961

Production company: Paramount Talent Associates. *Country:* U.S.A. *Distributed by:* Paramount. *Running time:* 98 minutes. *Producer:* David Susskind. *Associate producer:* Audrey Gellen. *Director:* Marc Daniels. *Technical director:* Lawrence Elikann. *Associate director:* Robert Hopkins. *Screenplay:* Dale Wasserman, *based on* Graham Greene's novel. *Photography:* Alan Posage, Leo Farrenkopf. *Editors:* Sidney Meyers, Walter Hess. *Art direction:* Burr Smidt. *Music:* Laurence Rosenthal. *Sound:* Frank Lewin, Albert Gramaglia. *Sound recording:* James Blaney.

CAST

Laurence Olivier	*The Priest*
Julie Harris	*Maria*
George C. Scott	*Police Lieutenant*
Roddy McDowell	*Peasant*
Keenan Wynn	*Bootlegger*
Patty Duke	*Coral*
Cyril Cusack	*Tench*
Martin Gabel	*Chief of Police*
Frank Conroy	*Padre Jose*
Mildred Dunnock	*Spinster*
Fritz Weaver	*Schoolmaster*

STORY

The last surviving priest in a Latin-American state, run by fiercely anti-Church revolutionaries, is relentlessly hunted by an avenging police lieutenant. A dissolute drunk, the priest is sheltered by the people of the village where the mother of his illegitimate child lives. He goes to the city, is arrested for buying forbidden liquor, but again escapes detection. He manages to flee across the frontier, where the prospect of an easy life as a practising priest tempts him. But he heeds the message of a dying man, returns across the frontier, is trapped by the police and faces a firing squad.

CRITICS' CIRCLE

"Apart from Laurence Olivier, who gives a magnetic performance as the priest, the rest of the cast figure briefly in dramatic highspots rather than as unobtrusive links in the narrative chain." — *The Daily Cinema*

"Unfortunately this muscular performance (of George C. Scott) tends to make Laurence Olivier's agonised martyr seem flabby and self-indulgent by comparison. There are signs of haste in shooting, the make-up is poor, the photographic quality hazy." — *Monthly Film Bulletin*

"Laurence Olivier has his moments as the decadent, though not completely damned priest, but George C. Scott creates a stronger impression as the police lieutenant. The supporting players are of little consequence." — *Kinematograph Weekly*

NOTES

This film was made for U.S. television but released (as a film) in Europe.

TERM OF TRIAL

1962

In and out of bed with Simone Signoret.

A Romulus Production, made at Ardmore Studios, Ireland. *Presented by:* Warner Bros. *Released through:* Warner-Pathe. *Country:* G.B. *Running time:* 130 minutes. *Producer:* James Woolf. *Written and directed by:* Peter Glenville, *based on the novel by:* James Barlow. *Photography:* Oswald Morris. *Production designer:* Wilfred Shingleton. *Associate producer:* James Ware. *Editor:* James Clark. *Continuity:* Phyllis Crocker. *Assistant director:* Gerald O'Hara. *Music composed by:* Jean-Michel Demase. *Conducted by:* W. Lambert Williamson. *Production manager:* Charles Blair. *Costume supervisor:* Beatrice Dawson. *Camera operator:* Brian West. *Sound mixer:* Charles Poulton and Len Shilton. *Dubbing editor:* Peter Musgrave. *Art director:* Antony Woolard. *Set dresser:* Peter James. *Make-up:* E. Gasser. *Hairdresser:* Gordon Bond.

CAST

Laurence Olivier	*Graham Weir*
Simone Signoret	*Anne*
Roland Culver	*Trowman*
Frank Pettingell	*Ferguson*
Thora Hird	*Mrs. Taylor*
Dudley Foster	*Dt. Sgt. Kiernan*
Norman Bird	*Mr. Taylor*
Newton Blick	*Prosecutor*
Allan Cuthbertson	*Sylvan Jones*
Nicholas Hannen	*Magistrate Sharp*
Roy Holder	*Thompson*
Barbara Ferris	*Joan*
Rosamund Greenwood	*Constance*
Lloyd Lamble	*Insp. Ullyatt*
Vanda Godsell	*Mrs. Thompson*
Earl Cameron	*Chard*
Clive Colin Bowler	*Collins*
Sarah Miles	*Shirley Taylor*
Hugh Griffith	*O'Hara*
Terence Stamp	*Mitchell*

Teacher and pupil: with Sarah Miles.

STORY

Graham Weir is a teacher at a secondary modern school in a North Country English town. He has been imprisoned as a conscientious objector during the war and so cannot get a better job — both of which facts cause his French wife, Anne, to nag him. Shirley Taylor, one of his pupils, falls in love with him and during a school trip to Paris attempts to seduce him. When he kindly but firmly rejects her, she turns against him and accuses him of assault. He is found guilty but the girl breaks down and tells the truth and the case is then dismissed.

CRITICS' CIRCLE

"The schoolmaster hero of *Term Of Trial* . . . offers this great player a framework for one of the finest portraits in his long, long gallery." — Paul Dehn, *Daily Herald*

"It is an excellent story that fails to make its full effect principally because of the miscasting of Sir Laurence, who seems to have a taste for playing insignificant little men, but his noble looks, his commanding personality and his natural authority are against him. He can play a king but he cannot play a mouse." — Thomas Wiseman, *Daily Express*

"It is not perhaps a fired performance, but it is minute and conscientious in its observation of the intelligent, blinkered sage and innocent schoolmaster with his diffident ways and his drab raincoat." — David Robinson, *Financial Times*

"If there is one role that Sir Laurence Olivier cannot play well, it is that of the little man. This pronunciamento — I'm afraid it sounds like that — is prompted by watching Olivier this week give a performance that reveals this cruel limitation to the finest tragic acting talent of his generation." — Alexander Walker, *Evening Standard*

NOTES

Both Laurence Olivier and Sarah Miles won top acting awards for this film at the Cork Film Festival for 1962. For Miss Miles and Terence Stamp it was a screen debut.

OTHELLO

1965

Production company: B.H.E. *Released through:* Eagle Films Ltd. *Country:* G.M. Panavision. Technicolor. *Producers:* Anthony Havelock-Allan and John Brabourne. *Director:* Stuart Burge. *Production:* As presented by the National Theatre of G.B. and directed on the stage by John Dexter. *Designed for the screen by:* William Kellner. *Based on the original National Theatre Designs by* Jocelyn Herbert. *Photography:* Geoffrey Unsworth. *Associate producer:* Richard Goodwin.

CAST

Laurence Olivier . . . .*Othello*
Maggie Smith. . . . .*Desdemona*
Joyce Redman. . . . .*Emilia*
Frank Finlay . . . . *Iago*
Derek Jacobi . . . .*Cassio*
Robert Lang . . . . *Roderigo*
Kenneth Mackintosh . . . .*Lodovico*
Anthony Nicholls . . . .*Brabantio*
Sheila Reid . . . . *Bianca*

STORY

William Shakespeare's tale of jealousy and revenge. Against her father's wishes Desdemona marries Othello, the Moor. His mind is poisoned by the cunning Iago and he murders his wife in a fit of unjustified jealousy.

CRITICS' CIRCLE

"His Othello, immensely theatrical, consciously created down to the last turn of a heel, the flicker of a finger, the shadow of an eyelid must now count among the world's great film performances." — John Mortimer, *The Observer*

"The stage and the cinema are very different media: the production which dazzles in the theatre can be heavy and muzzy on the screen; the performance which looks well from the stalls will not necessarily do so in close up: and this is a case in which, on the screen, one sees too much of the workings." — David Robinson, *Financial Times*

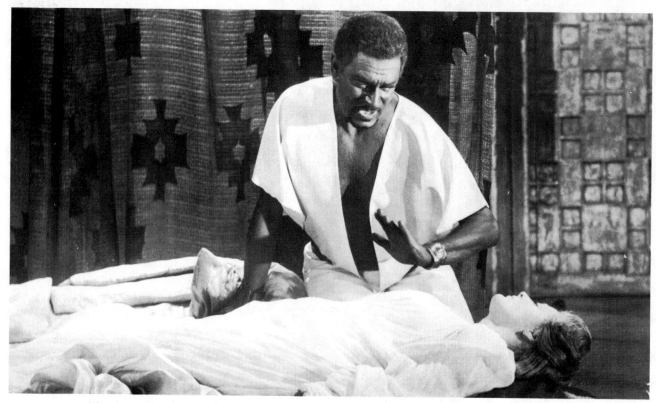

"Be thus when thou art dead and I will kill thee and love thee after": Maggie Smith as Desdemona

"Captured for future generations is Laurence Olivier's resonantly inventive creation of the Moor. In vocal performance it is as good as on the stage. Only the fact that the camera has to settle for the medium shots cuts it down slightly in dramatic stature — for Olivier acts the part from top to toe, not just to the waistline." — Alexander Walker, *Evening Standard*

"*Othello* with Laurence Olivier is a filmed record of the theatrical production; it would be our loss if we waited for posterity to discover it. Olivier's negro Othello — deep voice with a trace of foreign music in it, happy, thick, self-satisfied laugh; rolling buttocks; grand and barbaric and, yes, a little lewd — almost makes this great impossible play work. It has always made more than sense; now it almost makes sense, too — not only dramatic poetry, but a comprehensible play." — Pauline Kael, *New Yorker*

NOTES
This film won Olivier his seventh Academy Award nomination. It was banned for five years in South Africa since it concerned "love across the racial lines".

BUNNY LAKE IS MISSING

1965

A Columbia Release. Panavision. *Running time:* 107 minutes. *Producer and director:* Otto Preminger. *Associate producer:* Martin C. Schute. *Screenplay:* John and Penelope Mortimer, *based on a novel by:* Evelyn Piper. *Photography:* Denys Coop. *Music:* Paul Glass. *Production designer:* Don Ashton. *Make-up:* Neville Smallwood. *Hairdressing:* Maud Onslow. *Wardrobe mistress:* Evelyn Gibbs. *Wardrobe master:* Ray Beck. *Associate producer:* Martin C. Schute. *Assistant directors:* Bryan Coates, Bernie Williams and Ivor Nightingale. *Editor:* Peter Thornton. *Sound:* Claud Hitchcock, Red Law. *Sound editor:* Jonathan Bates. *Music editor:* Valerie Lesser. *Special effects:* Charles Staffell. *Set decorators:* Elven Webb, Scott Simon. *Titles:* Paul Bass.

CAST

Keir Dullea	*Steven Lake*
Carol Lynley	*Ann Lake*
Lucie Mannheim	*Cook*
Noël Coward	*Wilson*
Delphi Lawrence	*1st Mother*
Suzanne Neve	*2nd Mother*
Adrienne Corri	*Dorothy*
Kika Markham	*Nurse*
Jill Melford	*Teacher*
Anna Massey	*Elvira Smollet*
Martita Hunt	*Ada Ford*
Laurence Olivier	*Inspector Newhouse*
Clive Revill	*Sgt. Andrews*
Damaris Hayman	*Daphne*
Patrick Jordan	*Policeman*
Jane Evers	*Policewoman*
John Sharp	*Fingerprint man*
Geoffrey Frederick	*Police Photographer*
Percy Herbert	*Policeman at the Station*
Michael Wynne	*Rogers*
Bill Maxam	*Barman*
Tim Brinton	*Newscaster*
Themselves	*The Zombies*
Victor Maddern	*Taxi Driver*
Fred Emney	*Man in Soho*
Finlay Currie	*Doll Maker*
Richard Wattis	*Clerk in Shipping Office*
David Oxley	*Doctor*
John Forbes-Robertson	*Hospital attendant*
Megs Jenkins	*Sister*

STORY

When Ann Lake comes to a nursery school in Hampstead to collect her four-year-old daughter Bunny, she is unable to find her. There is no record of the child having been brought to the school, nor can Ann's brother Steven, an American journalist, cast any light on the mystery. Called to investigate, Inspector Newhouse of Scotland Yard is also unable to find any evidence that Bunny was ever enrolled at the school. He hints the whole story might be a figment of a young unmarried mother's imagination, even that Steven might be shielding his sister from a revelation that the child is illusory.

With Carol Lynley as Ann Lake.

But Ann insists the child is real and that she must be found before harm comes to her. At the mews flat which she and Steven have rented from Wilson, an eccentric and dissolute pseudo-intellectual, Ann becomes distraught as he bombards her with questions. Distractedly she searches for some clues which will prove Bunny's existence and finds the claim-ticket for a doll she has sent for repair. Steven has in fact kidnapped the child, as he is jealous of his sister's affection for her. He threatens both of them, but Inspector Newhouse realises the truth in time to save Ann and Bunny.

CRITICS' CIRCLE

". . . towering over the story (is) the police superintendent of Laurence Olivier: a performance almost self-effacing, but still massive, hinting force behind the official mask." — Dilys Powell, *Sunday Times*

". . . and Laurence Olivier with his towering technique of wit and timing makes this inspector one of the most beguiling policemen in the history of criminology." — Michael Thornton, *Sunday Express*

"Olivier is the man to watch. Instead of rounding out the flattish character of the inspector, he sits like a paper-weight on his own personality so that the character lies even flatter. Only a great actor dare make himself this small. It is a rare sight." — Alexander Walker, *Evening Standard*

"As the detective Olivier is flat-footed." — Leonard Mosley, *Daily Express*

"To keep an eye on everyone, there is the man from Scotland Yard — dryly played by Sir Laurence Olivier, who seems bemused to find his king-sized talent tucked into so mundane a role." — *Time*

NOTES

This was the first (and only other) time that Olivier and Coward had played together since their stage success in *Private Lives* in 1930.

With Anna Massey, Keir Dullea and Clive Revill

With Richard Wattis and Clive Revill.

140

KHARTOUM

1966

A Julian Blaustein Production. *Presented by:* Cinerama. *Released by:* United Artists. Technicolor. *Running time:* 128 minutes. *Producer:* Julian Blaustein. *Director:* Basil Dearden. *Screenplay:* Robert Ardrey. *Editor:* Fergus McDonell. *Production supervisor:* Charles Orme. *Photography:* Edward Scaifi. *Special effects:* Richard Parker. *Art director:* John Howell. *Prologue scenes directed by:* Eliot Elisofen. *Music composed and conducted by:* Frank Cordell. *Second unit director:* Yakima Canutt. *Second unit photography:* Harry Waxman. *Research:* Mary Bruce. *Special location consultant:* Major General S. E. Sabbour.

CAST

Charlton Heston . . . . *General Charles Gordon*
Laurence Olivier . . . . *The Mahdi*
Richard Johnson . . . . *Col. J. D. H. Stewart*
Ralph Richardson . . . . *Mr. Gladstone*
Alexander Knox . . . . *Sir Evelyn Baring*
Johnny Sekka . . . . *Khaleel*
Nigel Green . . . . *General Wolseley*
Michael Hordern . . . . *Lord Granville*
Zia Mohyeddin . . . .*Zobeir Pasha*
Hugh Williams . . . .*Lord Hartington*
Douglas Wilmer . . . .*The Khalifa Abdullah*
Edward Underdown . . . .*Col. Hicks*
Alec Mango . . . . *Bordeini Bey*
Jerome Willis . . . .*Frank Power*
Peter Arne . . . .*Major Kitchener*
Alan Tilvern . . . . *Awaan*
Michael Anthony . . . . *Herbin*
Marne Maitland . . . . *Sheikh Osman*
Leila . . . .*The Dancer*
Ronald Leigh-Hunt . . . .*Lord Northbrook*
Ralph Michael . . . .*Sir Charles Dilke*

STORY

After a British Colonel and his 10,000 untrained Egyptian troops are massacred by a fanatical Arab religious leader, the Mahdi, in the Sudan in 1883, General Charles Gordon, a national hero who has already spent six years in the country, is sent by Gladstone to evacuate the 13,000 troops in Khartoum and the civilians. But he is warned that his mission is unofficial so the government will not promise to back him up. Gordon is in fact in a hopeless situation. Khartoum falls to the Mahdi and Gordon is killed.

CRITICS' CIRCLE

"The only important drawback of the film, in fact, is the role of the Mahdi and the way it is played by Sir Laurence Olivier: we are given a formidable display of eye-rolling and lip-licking, a weird Peter Sellers oriental accent and a valiant but unsuccessful attempt to disguise Sir Laurence's all-too-English features with false hair and green lipstick. But no feeling of a real man ever comes over. Perhaps it is the difference between stage and film acting; no doubt Sir Laurence could act rings around Mr. Heston at the National Theatre, but here, as in that earlier and apparently just as unfair contest between Sir Laurence and Marilyn Monroe in *The Prince And The Showgirl*, there remains no doubt either about whose shadow has more substance on the silver screen." — *The Times*

"Olivier acts as brilliantly as one expected, altering Othello's basso profundo into a sing-song countertenor, sporting the lucky V-shape gap in his front teeth to show how well the film's researchers have done their work, and giving all place names their native pronunciation — 'Khartoum' sounds like a cough — to show how well he has done his research." — Alexander Walker, *Evening Standard*

". . . Olivier's Mahdi is a small masterpiece of single-minded religious insanity — the lambent black eyes never blinking, the measured voice conjuring up holy terrors from his private heart of darkness." — *Time*

NOTES

This film is generally acknowledged as more literate than the average epic, but was still blamed for being less than accurate. Olivier filmed the Mahdi immediately after his National Theatre Othello.

The Mahdi reads from The Koran

THE SHOES OF THE FISHERMAN

1968

A George Englund Enterprises Production. *Presented by:* MGM. *Released by:* MGM-EMI. Panavision. Metrocolor. *Running time:* 155 minutes. *Producer:* George Englund. *Director:* Michael Anderson. *Screenplay:* Morris West, *adapted from his own novel. Additional dialogue:* James Kennaway. *Photography:* Erwin Hillier. *Art director:* Edward Carfagno. *Production supervisor:* Stanley Goldsmith. *Production manager:* Danilo Sabatini. *Casting supervisor:* Irene Howard. *Costumes:* Orietta Nasalli-Rocca. *Sound recording:* Kurt Doubravsky. *Continuity:* Yvonne Axworthy. *Make-up:* Amato Garbini. *Hairstyles:* Gabriella Borzelli. *Assistant directors:* Tony Brandt, Victor Tourjansky. *Set dresser:* Arrigo Breschi. *Property master:* Elio Altamura. *Wardrobe supervisor:* Annalisa Nasalli-Rocca. *Music: Alex North.*

CAST

Anthony Quinn	*Kiril Lakota*
Oskar Werner	*David Telemond*
David Janssen	*George Faber*
Barbara Jefford	*Ruth Faber*
Leo McKern	*Cardinal Leone*
Vittorio De Sica	*Cardinal Rinaldi*
John Gielgud	*First Pope*
Clive Revill	*Vucovich*
Rosemary Dexter	*Chiara*
Paul Rogers	*Augustinian*
Niall MacGinnis	*Dominican*
Frank Finlay	*Yuri Bounin*
Burt Kwouk	*Peng*
George Pravda	*Gorshenin*
Arnoldo Foa	*Gelasio*
Arthur Howard	*English Cardinal*
Alfred Thomas	*Negro Cardinal*
Dom Moor	*Polish Cardinal*
John Frederick	*American Cardinal*
Laurence Olivier	*Kamenev*

STORY

Kiril Lakota, a Russian priest, is suddenly released from Siberia after twenty years' imprisonment and brought to Rome. The old and dying Pope who has arranged his release immediately creates him Cardinal. After the Pope dies, Kirk is acclaimed Pope by the College of Cardinals led by Cardinal Rinaldi. Kiril develops a friendship with Father Telemond, an unorthodox Jesuit. His relationship with Kamenev, the Russian premier who was once his hated interrogator, is renewed when Kamenev, anxious to avoid war with China, turns to Kiril, now spiritual leader of 800 million people, for help. Kiril gives away the wealth of the Church to the starving Chinese, thus averting World War III.

CRITICS' CIRCLE

"Lord Olivier strolls through his rôle as the Rus-

With Anthony Quinn

sian Premier who once imprisoned Quinn for 20 years — but I suppose it pays the rent." — Sue Freeman, *Daily Express*

"Olivier, along with Frank Finlay and Clive Revill, are superior in projecting not unsympathetic Russian politicians." — *Variety*

NOTES
It was immediately after this filming in Rome that Olivier openly admitted he had been living with a

diagnosis of cancer. "I said to myself, 'I will beat you, you bastard, and I have'."

The Shoes Of The Fisherman was not released in the U.K. until 1972. It was generally thought to be a well-meaning but implausible film — overly long and slow with all the actors struggling to bring life into it. The best scenes are the traditional Vatican ones of pomp and ceremony. Morris West later asked to have his screenplay credit removed from the film.

With Anthony Quinn and Oskar Werner

Discussing the script with director Michael Anderson

147

ROMEO AND JULIET

1968

Production company: Verona Productions/De Laurentiis Cine. *Released by:* Paramount. Technicolor. *Running time:* 152 minutes. *Producers:* Anthony Havelock-Allan, John Brabourne. *Associate producer:* Richard Goodwin. *Production manager:* Guisseppe Bordogni. *Director:* Franco Zeffirelli. *Assistant directors:* Isa Bartalini, Anna Davini, Dyson Lovell, Carlos Barbiere. *Screenplay:* Franco Brusati, Masolino D'Amica, *adapted from the play by* William Shakespeare. *Photography:* Pasquale De Santis. *Editor:* Reginald Mills. *Production designer:* Renzo Mongiardino. *Assistant designers:* Luciano Puccini, Emilio Carcano. *Set decoration:* Christine Edzard. *Music:* Nino Rota. *Lyrics:* Eugene Walter. *Costumes:* Danilo Donati. *Sound:* Sash Fisher.

CAST

Leonard Whiting . . . . *Romeo*
Olivia Hussey. . . . . *Juliet*
Milo O'Shea. . . . . *Friar Laurence*
Michael York. . . . . *Tybalt*
John McEnery . . . .*Mercutio*
Pat Heywood. . . . . *Nurse*
Natasha Parry . . . . *Lady Capulet*
Paul Hardwick. . . . . *Lord Capulet*
Robert Stephens . . . . *Prince of Verona*
Keith Skinner . . . . *Balthazar*
Richard Warwick. . . . . *Gregory*
Roberto Bisacco . . . .*Count Paris*
Bruce Robinson. . . . .*Benvolio*
Dyson Lovell. . . . .*Sampson*
Ugo Barbone . . . . *Abraham*
Antonio Pierfederici . . . . *Lord Montagu*
Esmeralda Ruspoli. . . . . *Lady Montagu*
Roy Halder . . . . *Peter*
Aldo Miranda . . . . *Friar John*
Dario Tanzini . . . . *Page to Tybalt*
Prologue and epilogue spoken by Laurence Olivier

STORY

Zeffirelli's screen treatment of Shakespeare's classic romance. In this version the greatest innovation is that the star-crossed lovers are indeed teenagers.

CRITICS' CIRCLE

"It is a trifle ironic that the only voice which seems able to take the measure of Shakespeare should be the one without a face — Laurence Olivier who speaks the prologue and epilogue." — Eric Shorter, *Daily Telegraph*

NOTES

Laurence Olivier took part in this film at his own request, so impressed was he with Zeffirelli's work for Olivier at the National Theatre. He was also unbilled at his own request.

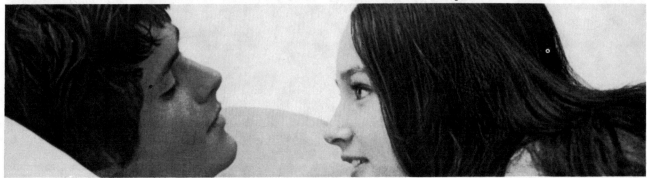

Leonard Whiting and Olivia Hussey

OH! WHAT A LOVELY WAR

1969

Production company: Accord/Paramount. *Distributed by:* Paramount. Panavision. Technicolor. *Running time:* 144 minutes. *Director:* Richard Attenborough. *Producers:* Brian Duffy and Richard Attenborough. *Associate producer:* Mack Davidson. *Photography:* Gerry Turpin. *Production designer:* Don Ashton. *The songs orchestrated and incidental music composed and conducted by:* Alfred Ralston. *Costume designer:* Anthony Mendelson. *Choreography:* Eleanor Fazan. *Editor:* Kevin Connor. *Assistant director:* Claude Watson. *Art director:* Harry White. *Set dresser:* Peter James. *Make-up supervisor:* Stuart Freeborn. *Chief hairdresser:* Biddy Chrystal. *Military adviser:* Major-General Sir Douglas Campbell KBE, CB, DSO, MC.

CAST

Ralph Richardson . . . .*Sir Edward Grey*
Meriel Forbes . . . . *Lady Grey*
Wensley Pithey . . . . . . *Archduke Franz Ferdinand*
Ruth Kettlewell. . . . . . . *Duchess Sophie, his wife*
Ian Holm. . . . . *President Poincaré*
John Gielgud. . . . .*Count Berchtold*
Kenneth More . . . . *Kaiser Wilhelm II*
John Clements. . . . .*General Von Moltke*
Paul Daneman . . . . *Tsar Nicholas II*
Joe Melia. . . . .*The Photographer*
Jack Hawkins . . . .*Emperor Franz Joseph*
John Hussey . . . .*Soldier on the balcony*
Kim Smith. . . . . *Dickie Smith*
Mary Wimbush . . . . *Mary Smith*
Paul Shelley. . . . .*Jack Smith*
Wendy Allnutt. . . . .*Flo Smith*
John Rae. . . . .*Grandpa Smith*
Kathleen Wileman . . . .*Emma Smith (aged 4)*
Corin Redgrave . . . .*Bertie Smith*
Malcolm McFee. . . . . *Freddie Smith*
Colin Farrell . . . .*Harry Smith*
Maurice Roeves. . . . .*George Smith*
Angela Thorne. . . . . *Betty Smith*

John Mills . . . .*Field Marshal Sir Douglas Haig*
Julia Wright. . . . .*His secretary*
Jean-Pierre Cassel . . . .*French Colonel*
Penny Allen. . . . .*Solo Chorus Girl*
Maggie Smith. . . . .*Music Hall Star*
David Lodge . . . . *Recruiting Sergeant*
Michael Redgrave . . . . . .*General Sir Henry Wilson*
Laurence Olivier . . . *Field-Marshal Sir John French*
Peter Gilmore . . . .*Private Burgess*
Derek Newark. . . . . . .*Shooting Gallery Proprietor*
Richard Howard . . . .*Young Soldier at Mons*
John Trigger . . . .*Office at station*
Ron Pember . . . .*Corporal at station*
Juliet Mills. . . . .*First Nurse at station*
Nanette Newman. . . . .*Second Nurse at station*
Susannah York . . . .*Eleanor*
Dirk Bogarde. *Stephen*
Cecil Parker. . . . . *Sir John*
Robert Flemyng . . . .*Staff Officer*
Thorley Walters. . . . . . .*1st staff officer (ballroom)*
Norman Shelley. . . . . .*2nd staff officer (ballroom)*

With Michael Redgrave

Sir Ralph Richardson, Sir John Gielgud and Kenneth More

Isabel Dean	*Sir John French's Lady*
Guy Middleton	*General Sir William Robertson*
Cecilia Darby.	*Sir Henry Wilson's Lady*
Natasha Parry	*Sir William Robertson's Lady*
Phyllis Calvert	*Lady Haig*
Raymond S. Edwards	*3rd staff officer*
Freddie Ascott	*"Whizzbang" soldier*
Edward Fox	*First Aide*
Geoffrey Davies.	*2nd Aide*
Vanessa Redgrave	*Sylvia Pankhurst*
Clifford Mollison.	*1st Heckler*
Dorothy Reynolds.	*2nd Heckler*
Harry Locke	*3rd Heckler*
George Ghent	*4th Heckler*
Michael Bates	*Drunken Lance Corporal*
Charles Farrell.	*Policeman*
Fanny Carby	*1st Mill Girl*
Marianne Stone	*2nd Mill Girl*
Christine Noonan	*3rd Mill Girl*
Charlotte Attenborough . . .	*Emma Smith (aged 8)*

STORY

This film underlines the horror of the First World War in a highly stylized compilation of songs and quotes for the period. The action is focussed on the Smith family whose sons go off to war and are killed. Laurence Olivier portrays Field-Marshal Sir John French.

CRITICS' CIRCLE

"The knights of English acting (Richardson, Red-grave, Clements, Gielgud and Olivier) take their places as diplomats or warlords and allow Olivier as Field Marshal Sir John French, to steal the scenes away in a brief but brilliant performance." — Ann Pacey, *Sun*

"Laurence Olivier is a finely comic French." — David Robinson, *Financial Times*

". . . Olivier's brandy-logged Sir John French must be singled out." — Kenneth Allsop, *Observer*

"The funniest knight of all is Sir Laurence Olivier's Sir John French twitching his stiff white moustache as he asks Haig: 'Tell me Douglas, what d'you think of this fellow Kitchener?'." — Cecil Wilson, *Daily Mail*

NOTES

This film was based on Joan Littlewood's 1963 stage production which in turn was based on a radio programme of 1914-1918 soldiers' songs compiled by Charles Chilton in *The Long Long Trail*.

The Society of Film and Television Arts gave the film its United Nations award and gave Laurence Olivier the award as best supporting actor.

"Well, the key was Larry. He knew this was my first film as a director and because he is one of the nicest men in the world he agreed to play a small part." — Richard Attenborough.

With John Mills

THE DANCE OF DEATH

1969

Production company: BHE/National Theatre Company Production for Paramount. *Country:* G.B. Technicolor. *Running time:* 148 minutes. *Producer:* John Brabourne. *Director:* David Giles. *Associate producer:* Richard Goodwin. *Photography:* Geoffrey Unsworth. *Art director:* Herbert Smith. *Editor:* Reginald Mills. *Translated by:* C. D. Locock. *From the play by:* August Strindberg. *Production manager:* Elisabeth Woodthorpe. *Set decorations:* Helen Thomas. *Costumes:* Amy C. Binney. *Sound:* John Aldred.

CAST

Laurence Olivier	*Edgar*
Geraldine McEwan	*Alice*
Robert Lang	*Kurt*
Carolyn Jones	*Jenny*
Maggie Riley	*Kristin*
Jeanne Watts	*Old Woman*
Janina Faye	*Judith*
Malcolm Reynolds	*Allan*
Peter Penry-Jones	*Lieutenant*
Frederick Pyne, Barry James, David Ryall	*Sentries*

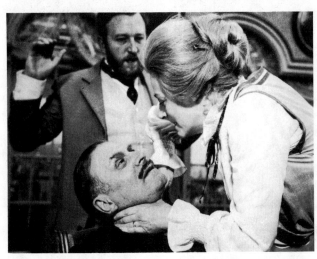

With Geraldine McEwan and Robert Lang

STORY

Edgar, an artillery captain, and his wife Alice live isolated from social contact on an island fortress off the Swedish coast. They bicker and argue constantly and Edgar refuses to admit that he is a sick man. Alice's cousin, Kurt, comes to the island as Quarantine Officer and the Captain ruins him socially and financially as well as professionally. But Edgar's daughter falls in love with Kurt's son and insults the old general to whom she is engaged. Edgar dies from a stroke brought on by the shock.

CRITICS' CIRCLE

"Huge close-ups reveal the smallest mechanics and calculations of every performance . . . Microphones amplify each word with no apparent attempt at balance so that everyone seems to be shouting his head off — particularly disastrous in the case of Olivier, who uses a staccato military bark that shatters the eardrums . . . One remembers the fascinating ebb and flow of the personal conflict, the unexpectedly frequent laughter and the almost reluctant compassion of the stage version. And knowing what a superb film actor Olivier can be, one regrets more than ever that this extraordinary performance should have been committed to celluloid as a travesty of itself." — Brenda Davies, *Monthly Film Bulletin*

"Sir Laurence's performance is dismaying to a degree one would not have thought possible. It is a performance which is compounded of every showoffy gimmick he has ever picked up; he never stops winking, as it were, at the audience; and is not surprising that he is therefore totally unconvincing." — Richard Roud, *The Guardian*

"One of Laurence Olivier's greatest performances — perhaps his greatest — has been encapsulated in a tin can for posterity. Surely that should be enough?" — Penelope Mortimer, *The Observer*

With Geraldine McEwan

With Robert Lang

"Olivier's Edgar is unquestionably one of his very best recent performances, viciously comic, painfully truthful. Much of it is only more fascinating when magnified by the camera; yet equally, the camera at times shows up the mechanics of calculation, the self-consciousness of some of his theatrical 'moments', the occasional retreats into elocutionary devices to cover weaknesses of interpretation." — David Robinson, *Financial Times*

"Everytime we single out the feature that makes Olivier a marvel — his lion eyes or the voice or the way it seizes on a phrase — he alters it or casts it off in some new rôle, and is greater than ever. It is no special asset, it is the devilish audacity and courage of this man . . . What is extraordinary is inside, and what is even more extraordinary is his determination to give it outer force. He has never levelled off; he goes on soaring." — Pauline Kael

Edgar, the embittered army captain, suffers a stroke

THE BATTLE OF BRITAIN

1969

Production company: Spitfire Productions Ltd. *Released by:* United Artists. Panavision and Technicolor. *Running time:* 131 minutes. *Producers:* Harry Saltzman and S. Benjamin Fisz. *Director:* Guy Hamilton. *Screenplay:* James Kennaway, S. Benjamin Fisz. *Photography:* Freddie Young. *Music composed by:* Sir William Walton O.M. *Conducted by:* Malcolm Arnold. *Associate producer:* John Palmer. *Production supervisor:* Sydney Streeter. *Supervising art director:* Maurice Carter. *Art directors:* Bert Davey, Jack Maxsted, William Hutchinson, Gil Parrondo. *Special effects:* Cliff Richardson, Glen Robinson, Wally Veevers, Ray Caple. *Assistant director:* Derek Cracknell. *Aerial and 2nd unit director:* David Bracknell. *2nd unit director and photography:* Skeets Kelly, John Jordan. *Continuity:* Elaine Schreyeck. *Editor:* Bert Bates. *Sound editors:* James Shields, Ted Mason. *Sound:* Gordon Everett, Gordon McCallum. *British technical and tactical advisers:* Gp.Capt. Hamish Mahaddie, Gp.Capt. Tom Gleave, Wg.Cdr. Robert Wright, Wg.Cdr. Robert Standord-Tuck, Sq. Ldr. Ginger Lacey, Sq. Ldr. B. Drobinski, Wg.Cdr. Claire Legge (W.R.A.F.). *German technical and tactical advisers:* Lt.General Adolf Galland, Colonel Hans Brustellin, Major Franz Frodl.

With Michael Redgrave, discussing pilot training

CAST

Harry Andrews	Senior Civil Servant
Michael Caine	Sqd.Ldr. Canfield
Trevor Howard	Air Vice Marshal Keith Park
Curt Jurgens	Baron von Richter
Ian McShane	Sgt. Pilot Andy
Kenneth More	Group Capt. Baker
Laurence Olivier	Air Chief Marshal Sir Hugh Dowding
Nigel Patrick	Group Capt. Hope
Christopher Plummer	Sq.Ldr. Harvey
Michael Redgrave	Air Vice Marshal Evill
Ralph Richardson	British Minister in Switzerland
Robert Shaw	Sq.Ldr. Skipper
Patrick Wymark	Air Vice Marshal Trafford Leigh-Mallory
Susannah York	Section Officer Maggie Harvey
Michael Bates	Warrant Officer Warrick
Isla Blair	Andy's wife
John Bascomb	Farmer
Tom Chatto	Willoughby's Asst. Controller
James Cosmo	Jamie
Robert Flemyng	Wing Commander Willoughby
Barry Foster	Sq.Ldr. Edwards
Edward Fox	Pilot Officer Archie
W. G. Foxley	Sq.Ldr. Evans
David Griffin	Sgt. Pilot Chris
Jack Gwillim	Senior Air Staff Officer
Myles Hoyle	Peter
Duncan Lamont	Flt.Sgt. Arthur
Sarah Lawson	Skipper's wife
Mark Mahez	Pasco
André Maranne	French N.C.O.
Anthony Nichols	A minister
Nicholas Pennell	Simon
Andrzey Scibor	Ox
Jean Wladon	Jean-Jacques
Wilfried van Aacken	General Osterkamp
Karl Otto Alberty	Jeschonnek, Chief of Staff Luftwaffe
Alexander Allerson	Major Brandt
Dietrich Frauboes	Feldmarschall Milch
Alf Jungermann	Brandt's navigator
Peter Hager	Feldmarschall Kesselring

Wolf Harnish	*General Fink*
Reinhard Horras	*Bruno*
Helmut Kircher	*Boehm*
Paul Newhaus	*Major Foehn*
Malte Petzel	*Beppo Schmid*
Manfred Reddemann	*Major Falke*
Hein Reiss	*Reichmarschall Goering*
Rolf Stiefel	*Hitler*

STORY

This is a reconstruction of the war in the air over Britain in 1940. It covers a period of sixteen weeks in the summer of that year when Britain waited for the Nazi offensive from Europe. Laurence Olivier plays Sir Hugh Dowding who was the Commander-in-Chief of Fighter Command. Arguments over tactics for the air defence of Britain boiled down to the essential problem, a shortage of pilots. But pilots were desperately trained and when on September 15 Goering ordered the biggest onslaught ever, the tide began to turn in favour of Britain.

CRITICS' CIRCLE

"Take any five minutes of dog-fights over the Channel and the film looks marvellous. But five minutes is long enough: one plane going down in flames is very much like another, the people inside the planes are largely unrecognisable behind their masks, and though possibly to the expert eye the pilots perform prodigies of daring, to the uninitiated it all looks much the same . . . Only Sir Laurence Olivier is memorable, but then Sir Hugh Dowding is the only really written character, a dry, sad man who commands belief . . . Otherwise it is a long slow pull . . . Plane spotters will have a field day, but I'm not sure about less dedicated mortals." — John Russell Taylor, *The Times*

NOTES

"A film of this size is always difficult to cast because there are so many vital roles; because of the nature of important roles it becomes extremely hard to schedule, to slot in an actor's availability. This was our problem. Now we have succeeded. These are the best actors for the roles. Their names enhance our film, although the real star of the film is the story itself. Five units are working simultaneously to encompass the scope of the story: more than a hundred Spitfires, Hurricanes, Messerschmitts and Heinkels of the period have been assembled for the film." — Harry Saltzman, producer.

158

WL 141612

DAVID COPPERFIELD

1969

Production company: Omnibus. *Released by:* 20th Century Fox. Eastman Color. *Country:* U.K. *Running time:* 118 minutes. *Producer:* Frederick H. Brogger. *Assistant to producer:* Stuart Elliot. *Director:* Delbert Mann. *Associate producer:* Hugh Attwooll. *Screenplay:* Jack Pulman, *from the novel by:* Charles Dickens. *Assistant director:* Dominic Fulford. *Photography:* Ken Hodges. *Art director:* Alex Vetchinsky. *Assistant art director:* Brian Herbert. *Costume designer:* Anthony Mendleson. *Wardrobe master:* Brian Owen-Smith. *Wardrobe mistress:* Laurel Stafell. *Chief make-up:* Billy Partleton. *Chief hairdresser:* Elsie Alder. *Stills cameraman:* George Courtenay Ward. *Dialogue director:* James Seymour. *Editor:* Peter Boita. *Assistant editor:* Geoffrey Brown.

With Richard Attenborough

CAST

Robin Phillips	*David Copperfield*
Susan Hampshire	*Agnes Wickfield*
Edith Evans	*Betsy Trotwood*
Michael Redgrave	*Mr. Peggotty*
Ralph Richardson	*Mr. Micawber*
Wendy Hiller	*Mrs. Micawber*
Corin Redgrave	*Steerforth*
Pamela Franklin	*Dora*
Ron Moody	*Uriah Heep*
James Donald	*Mr. Murdstone*
Emlyn Williams	*Mr. Dick*
Laurence Olivier	*Mr. Creakle*
Richard Attenborough	*Mr. Tungay*
Megs Jenkins	*Clara Peggotty*
Anna Massey	*Jane Murdstone*
Cyril Cusack	*Barkis*
Nicholas Pennell	*Traddles*
Sinead Cusack	*Emily*
Andrew McCulloch	*Ham*
Isobel Black	*Clara Copperfield*
Donald Layne-Smith	*Mr. Wickfield*
James Hayter	*Porter*
Helen Cotterill	*Mary Ann*
Kim Craik	*Child Emily*
Alistair Mackenzie	*Child David*
Christopher Moran	*Boy Steerforth*
Jeffrey Chandler	*Boy Traddles*
Brian Tipping	*Boy*
Alison Blair	*Girl*
Liam Redmond	*Mr. Quinion*
Gordon Rollings	*Milkman*
George Woodbridge	*Vicar*
William Lyon-Brown	*Doctor*
Christine Ozanne	*Midwife*
Phoebe Shaw	*Prostitute*
Robert Lankesheer	*Mr. Sharp*
Ann Stallybrass	*Martha*

STORY

This is based on the classic novel by Charles Dickens. In this film version the story is told in flashback. Copperfield remembers his cruel stepfather, the odious schoolmasters Creakle and Tungay, and the boys who later became his companions, as he wanders along a bleak seashore.

BEWARE
THIS DOG.
HE BITES!

With Richard Attenborough

RICHARD ATTENBOROUGH · CYRIL CUSACK
EDITH EVANS · PAMELA FRANKLIN · SUSAN HAMPSHIRE
WENDY HILLER · RON MOODY · LAURENCE OLIVIER
ROBIN PHILLIPS · MICHAEL REDGRAVE
RALPH RICHARDSON · EMLYN WILLIAMS

IN CHARLES DICKENS'

David Copperfield

RICHARD ATTENBOROUGH as TUNGAY   CYRIL CUSACK as Mr. BARKIS

Produced by FREDERICK BROGGER · Directed by DELBERT MANN · Screenplay by JACK PULMAN

CRITICS' CIRCLE
"Laurence Olivier is allowed a moment or two of glory as Mr. Creakle, hilariously accompanied by a peg-legged Richard Attenborough as Mr. Tungay." — Derek Malcolm, *The Guardian*

"Laurence Olivier and Richard Attenborough's outrageous Creakle and Tungay double-act would have brought down the house closing the bill at the New Cross Empire." — Margaret Hinxman, *Sunday Telegraph*

"As for the ferocious headmaster, Mr. Creakle, hardly have we seen through another of Sir Laurence Olivier's marvellous disguises before he is gone." — Cecil Wilson, *Daily Mail*

"Laurence Olivier as Creakle has the menace of distant thunder." — Dilys Powell, *Sunday Times*

"Laurence Olivier and Richard Attenborough are a perfect Dickensian double act." — Alexander Walker, *Evening Standard*

NOTES
This production was made for U.S. television and released in Europe through cinemas. There had been several silent versions of *David Copperfield* as well as George Cukor's classic 1934 production.

162

THREE SISTERS

1970

Production company: Alan Clore Films/British Lion. *Distributed by:* Lion International Films Ltd. Eastman Color. *Country:* U.K. *Running time:* 165 minutes. *Director:* Laurence Olivier. *Co-director:* John Sichel. *Producer:* John Goldstone. *Executive producer:* Alan Clore. *Screenplay:* Moura Budberg, *from the play by* Anton Chekhov. *Editor:* Jack Harris. *Associate producers:* Timothy Burrill, James Shields. *Sound recordists:* Buster Ambler, Bob Jones. *Make-up:* Bob Lawrence, Philip Leakey. *Hairdressers:* Gladys Leakey, Carol Beckett. *Wardrobe mistress:* Jackie Breed. *Main musical themes arranged and composed by:* Sir William Walton O.M. *Other arrangements by:* Derek Hudson and Gary Hughes. *Conductor:* Marc Wilkinson. *Photography:* Geoffrey Unsworth. *Production designer:* Joseph Svoboda. *Art director:* Bill Hutchinson. *Assistant director:* Simon Relph. *Assistant art directors:* Peter Howitt, Timothy Bryan. *Scenic artist:* Gillian Noyes. *Assistant editor:* Hazel Wilkinson. *Titles:* Carvel.

CAST

Jeanne Watts . . . . *Olga (the eldest sister)*
Joan Plowright . . . . *Masha (the married sister)*
Louise Purnell . . . . *Irina (the youngest sister)*
Derek Jacobi . . . . *Andrei (their brother)*
Sheila Reid . . . . *Natasha (his wife)*
Kenneth Mackintosh . . *Kulighin (Masha's husband)*
Daphne Heard . . . . . . *Anfissa (the sister's old nana)*
Harry Lomax . . . . *Ferrapont (old watchman)*
Judy Wilson . . . . *Serving Maid*
Mary Griffiths . . . . *Housemaid*
Ronald Pickup . . . . *Tusenbach (the Baron)*
Laurence Olivier . . . . *Chebutikin (the Doctor)*
Frank Wylie . . . . . *Vassili Vassilich Solloni (Major)*
Alan Bates . . . . *Vershinin (the Colonel)*
Richard Kay . . . . *Fedotik (lieutenant)*
David Belcher . . . . *Rode(lieutenant)*
George Selaway . . . . *Orderly*
David Munro, Alan Adams,
Robert Walker . . . . *Officers*

With Daphne Heard in the sisters' drawing room

Olivier directs his wife Joan Plowright who plays Masha

Directing Joan Plowright and Alan Bates

STORY

The action of Anton Chekhov's classic play takes place in a Russian provincial town at the turn of the century. The three sisters and their brother have but one wish — to return to the intellectual pursuits and sophisticated atmosphere of Moscow. On Irina's Saint's Day the family are joined at a celebration lunch by Army officers from a local battery. Chebutikin, the doctor and an old family friend, is there too, as also are Solloni and Baron Tusenbach who are both in love with Irina. A fresh face appears, the new battery commander, Vershinin, and the party is completed with the arrival of Masha's husband Kulighin and an unsophisticated local girl, Natasha. Two years elapse. Andrei now works for the local council. He and Natasha are married, unhappily, and Natasha is running the household to suit herself. It is clear that Masha and Vershinin (who has a sick wife) have fallen in love.

Both Tusenbach and Solloni declare their love to an indifferent Irina. Some months later, after a fire, Natasha quarrels with her sisters-in-law. The old doctor gets drunk. Olga advises Irina to marry Tusenbach and she agrees too but he is killed by Solloni in a duel. The military get transferred and Masha breaks down as Vershinin leaves but is comforted by her husband. Olga says, "Our life has not yet come to an end. Let us live! Perhaps in a little while we will know why we live, why we suffer."

CRITICS' CIRCLE

". . . it is on the mere margin of cinema. The characters may move in a space beyond the compass of the stage; the camera, following them, may isolate their gestures and their expressions in a way impossible to the theatre, but the general effect is of projection in the theatrical sense . . . and many of the performances, among them Olivier's as Chebutikin, are to be admired — but it does not belong to the cinema." — Dilys Powell, *Sunday Times*

". . . it is a useful substitute for those who missed the play." — Margaret Hinxman, *Sunday Telegraph*

"Chekhov becomes the screen better than most playwrights. His plays are cinematic . . ." — Alexander Walker, *Evening Standard*

". . . is a beautiful piece of work, subtle, sensitive and deeply moving. It is far more than a photographed stage play." — Felix Barker, *Evening News*

"On only two significant occasions does Olivier depart from the stage version. Firstly for a rather flat fantasy sequence before Act IV in which Irina dreams of a beautiful future in Moscow and secondly when a flash-forward to the fatal duel is cut into the dialogue between Irina and the Baron. Frankly the picture — for all its manifest respectability and understandable reverence for the text — strikes me as a misguided enterprise confirming the belief that Chekhov's full-length plays (unlike his fiction) are unfilmable." — Philip French, *The Times*

NOTES

This is the first film Laurence Olivier had directed since *The Prince and the Showgirl.* It was adapted from his National Theatre production, seen at the Old Vic in the previous year.

Olivier grew a beard and moustache for the role of the doctor. "It is because I am the director that I decided to grow the beard," he explained. "It saves me an hour in the make-up chair each morning and I use the time to work out the day's scenes. For the same reason, I wear no make-up at all."

(L to R): Judy Wilson, Jeanne Watts, Alan Bates, Frank Wylie, Sheila Reid, Kenneth Mackintosh, Laurence Olivier, Louise Purnell, Ronald Pickup, David Belcher, Derek Jacobi, and Joan Plowright

NICHOLAS AND ALEXANDRA

1971

A Sam Spiegel — Franklin J. Schaffner Production. A Horizon Film from Columbia Pictures. *Country:* U.K. *Released by:* Columbia — Warner Distributors Ltd. Panavision Colour. *Running time:* 189 minutes. *Producer:* Sam Spiegel. *Director:* Franklin J. Schaffner. *Screenplay:* James Goldman, *from the book by:* Robert K. Massie. *Production designer and second unit director:* John Box. *Photography:* Freddie Young. *Music composed by:* Richard Rodney Bennett. *Associate producer:* Andrew Donally. *Costume designer:* Yvonne Blake. *Costumes for "Alexandra" and "Maria Fedorovna":* Antonio Castillo. *Film editor:* Ernest Walter. *Production supervisor:* Luis Roberts. *Second unit cameraman.* Manuel Berenguer. *Dialogue coordinator.* David Giles. *Additional dialogue:* Edward Bond. *Assistant director:* Jose Lopez Rodero. *Sound recordists:* George Stephenson, Gerry Humphreys. *Sound editor:* Winston Ryder. *Make-up:* Neville Smallwood. *Hairdressing:* A. G. Scott. *Wardrobe supervisors:* Betty Adamson, John Wilson Apperson. *Additional music arranged and conducted by:* Christopher Gunning. *Art directors:* Jack Maxsted, Ernest Archer, Gil Parrondo. *Assistant art directors:* Bob Laing, Alan Roderick-Jones. *Set dresser:* Vernon Dixon. *Property master and special effects:* Eddie Fowlie. *Uniform and Military advisor:* John Mollo. *Second unit costumes:* Anthony Powell. *Music performed by:* The New Philharmonia Orchestra of London. *Conducted by:* Marcus Dods.

CAST

The Royal Family

Michael Jayston	*Nicholas*
Janet Suzman	*Alexandra*
Roderick Noble	*Alexis*
Anita Marson	*Olga*
Lynne Frederick	*Tatiana*
Candace Glendenning	*Marie*
Fiona Fullerton	*Anastasia*
Harry Andrews	*Grand Duke Nicholas (Nikilasha)*
Irene Worth	*The Queen Mother Marie Fedorovna*

The Royal Household

Tom Baker	*Rasputin*
Jack Hawkins	*Count Fredericks*
Timothy West	*Dr. Botkin*
Katharine Schofield	*Tegleva*
Jean-Claude Drouot	*Gilliard*
John Hallam	*Nagorny*
Guy Rolfe	*Dr. Federov*
John Wood	*Col. Kobylinsky*

The Statesmen

Laurence Olivier	*Count Witte*
Eric Porter	*Stolypin*
Michael Redgrave	*Sazonov*
Maurice Denham	*Koboutsov*
Ralph Truman	*Rodzianko*
Gordon Gostelow	*Guchkov*
John McEnery	*Kerensky*

The Revolutionaries

Michael Bryant	*Lenin*
Vivian Pickles	*Mme. Krupskaya*
Brian Cox	*Trotsky*
James Hazeldine	*Stalin*
Stephen Greif	*Martov*
Steven Berkoff	*Pankratov*
Eric Chapman	*Plekhanov*
Ian Holm	*Yakovlev*
Alan Webb	*Yurosky*
Leon Lissek	*Avadeyev*
David Giles	*Goloshchekin*

Other Characters

Roy Dotrice	*General Alexeiev*
Martin Potter	*Prince Yussoupov*
Richard Warwick	*Grand Duke Dmitry*
Vernon Dobtcheff	*Dr. Lazovert*
Alexander Knox	*American Ambassador Root*
Ralph Neville	*British Ambassador Buchanan*
Jorge Rigaud	*French Ambassador Paleologue*
Curt Jurgens	*German Consul Sklarz*
Julian Glover	*Gapon*
John Shrapnel	*Petya*
Diana Quick	*Sonya*
John Forbes Robertson	*Col. Voikov*
Alan Dalton	*Flautist*
Penny Sugg	*Young Opera Singer*

Begging his Tsar not to fight

STORY

This is the story of the Russian revolution, seen in contrast through the domestic tragedy of the Tsar's family. Alexandra, distraught about her son's haemophilia, places trust in the monk Rasputin when the medical profession can offer her no hope. As she concentrates solely on her son, the feelings of the people and the court are ignored and hate for the royal family festers.

CRITICS' CIRCLE

"Eric Porter and Laurence Olivier are impressive as the Prime Ministers Stolypin and Count Witte. The tone of the film, directed by Franklin J. Schaffner, is one of earnestness and sincerity and while I admired it I was never very excited by it." — Ian Christie, *Daily Express*

". . . Count Witte (is) played with electrifying weariness by Olivier." — John Coleman, *New Statesman*

"Only Sir Laurence Olivier manages to pierce the pantomime by inventing details of performance that trick us into feeling for a moment." — Gavin Millar, *The Listener*

"Among the distinguished supporting players only Laurence Olivier as Sergei Witte has authority enough to fix attention on the character rather than on the Lord." — David Robinson, *Financial Times*

NOTES

This film won 1972 American Academy Awards for Art Direction, Set Decoration and Costume Design.

commanders round the war table

LADY CAROLINE LAMB

1972

Production company: An Anglo-EMI Film Distributor Ltd. Production (GEC/Pulsar Productions of London/Vidas Cinematografica, Rome for Anglo-EMI). *Released by:* MGM-EMI. *Running time:* 122 minutes. *Writer and director:* Robert Bolt. *Producer:* Fernando Ghia. *Executive producer:* Franco Cristaldi. *Associate producer:* Bernard Williams. *Editor:* Norman Savage. *Photography:* Oswald Morris. *Art director:* Carmen Dillon. *Costume designer;* David Walker. *Assistant director:* David Tringham. *Second assistant director:* Michael Stevenson. *Camera operator:* Jim Turrell. *Continuity:* June Randall. *Make-up:* George Frost. *Hairdresser:* Bobbie Smith. *Wardrobe supervisor:* Ron Beck. *Location manager:* Terence Clegg. *Set dresser:* Vernon Dixon. *Assistant art director:* Russel Hagg. *Second unit cameraman:* Paddy Carey. *Fight arranger:* Bob Simmons. *Sound recordist:* Bill Daniels. *Assistant editor:* Tony Lawson. *Sound editor:* Teddy Mason. *Music:* Richard Rodney Bennett. *Played by:* Peter Mark, solo viola. with the New Philharmonia Orchestra. *Conducted by:* Marcus Dods. *Dance movement:* Eleanor Fazan.

CAST

Sarah Miles	*Lady Caroline*
Jon Finch	*William Lamb*
Richard Chamberlain	*Lord Byron*
John Mills	*Canning*
Margaret Leighton	*Lady Melbourne*
Pamela Brown	*Lady Bessborough*
Ralph Richardson	*King George IV*
Laurence Olivier	*Duke of Wellington*
Sonia Dresdel	*Lady Pont*
Michael Wilding	*Lord Holland*
Fanny Rowe	*Lady Holland*
Silvia Monti	*Miss Milbanke*
Joyce Carey	*Marquise*
Maureen Pryor	*Mrs. Buller*
Peter Bull	*Government Minister*
Bernard Kay	*Benson*
Charles Carson	*Mr. Potter*
John Moffatt	*Murray*
Preston Lockwood	*1st Partner*
John Rapley	*2nd Partner*
Nicholas Field	*St. John*
Stephen Sheppard	*Buckham*
Trevor Peacock	*Agent*
Janet Key	*Miss Fairfax*
Ivor Slater	*Chatsworth Domo*
Ralph Truman	*Admiral*
Felicity Gibson	*Girl in Blue*
Robert Mill	*ADC to Wellington*

With Sarah Miles

STORY

Lady Caroline, a wild, romantic girl, marries up and-coming politician William Lamb. She then falls passionately in love with Lord Byron and her reckless indiscretions put her husband's career in jeopardy. When Byron tires of her she attempts suicide and then goes into a deep depression. At one point she decides to further her husband's career by seducing the Duke of Wellington. In the end she separates from Lamb for his own good and dies romantically in the garden at the dead of night.

CRITICS' CIRCLE

"Olivier electrifies his scenes as the Duke, basking in battlefield victory yet half-smothered by peace-time affectations and importunate favour-seekers . . . Olivier can even get eloquence into a groan." — Alexander Walker, *Evening Standard*

". . . Laurence Olivier's brief appearance as the Duke of Wellington (is) a beautifully witty and rounded characterisation that is worth the price of admission in itself." — Philip French, *The Times*

NOTES

This was Robert Bolt's first picture as director.
It was slammed by some for historical inaccuracies and often wishy-washy romanticism, but still accepted by others as a valid example of the historical-romantic genre.

SLEUTH

1973

Production company: Palomar Pictures International. *Released by:* Fox-Rank Distributors. *Country:* U.S. *Running time:* 138 minutes. *Executive producer:* Edgar J. Scherick. *Producer:* Morton Gottlieb. *Director:* Joseph L. Mankiewicz. *Screenwriter:* Anthony Shaffer, *based upon his own stage play. Associate producer:* David Middleman. *Photography:* Oswald Morris. *Production designer:* Ken Adam. *Music composer, conductor and arranger:* John Addison. *Art director:* Peter Lamont. *Film editor:* Richard Morden. *Assistant director:* Kip Furniss. *Production manager:* Frank Ernst. *Sound:* John Mitchell. *Set decoration:* John Jarvis. *Camera operator:* Jimmy Turrell. *Continuity:* Elaine Schreyeck. *Make-up:* Tom Smith. *Hairdresser:* Joan White. *Stills:* George Whitear.

CAST

Laurence Olivier .... *Andrew Wyke*
Michael Caine .... *Milo Tindle*
Alec Cawthorne. .... *Inspector Doppler*
Margo Channing .... *Marguerite*
John Matthews .... *Det. Sgt. Tarrant*
Teddy Martin .... *Police Constable Higgs*

STORY

Andrew Wyke, a distinguished detective novelist and inveterate games player, invites to his home in the country a young neighbour, Milo Tindle. During the evening Wyke tells him he knows that Milo is having an affair with his wife but assures him he does not mind at all — in fact he has an idea which will help Milo take his wife away and support her in the style to which she has become accustomed. They will fake a burglary. Milo will go off with the wife and her jewels and Wyke will collect the insurance. Then twist upon countertwist ensues with, at the end, Milo dead and Wyke awaiting the police to come and arrest him for the murder.

With Michael Caine

CRITICS' CIRCLE

"Wyke is not only wealthy, urbane, a connoisseur of mechanical toys and a master of the sardonic epigrams; he also provides Laurence Olivier with the best comedy role of his film career." — Felix Barker, *Evening News*

". . . I don't find that Sir Laurence Olivier and Michael Caine have improved matters on the screen. Actually, Olivier's vocal imitations are less accomplished than Peter Sellers', but I suppose we are supposed to be overwhelmed simply because Sir Laurence deigned to do them." — Andrew Sarris, *Village Voice*

"Olivier is quite brilliant, bounding athletically up and down baronial stairways and cellar steps and impressing his own authority on glib lines . . ." — Cecil Wilson, *Daily Mail*

"Sir Laurence Olivier is called on to act a theatrical character in a theatrical film. He subdues the theatrical element, but not so much as to disturb the artifices of the narrative; and we are left with a performance of exquisite professionalism, the portrait of a middle-aged literary show-off — defensively vain, finicky, waspish, with the cruelty and the concealed self-doubts of the solitary. To see him deliberately fixing himself a caviare snack is in itself a pleasure . . . But without him the film would be an uncomfortably gruesome bag of tricks." — Dilys Powell, *Sunday Times*

NOTES

This is a two-character film full of literary and celluloid cross-references. Margo Channing, who is given billing, is the character Bette Davis played in *All About Eve*, also directed by Mankiewicz.
Laurence Olivier was again nominated (his eighth time) for an Academy Award as best actor in 1973

— the award was won by Marlon Brando for *The Godfather*. Wyke was the first original leading role Olivier had played on the screen since *Khartoum* (1966) and it marked his return to the life of a freelance actor after nearly a decade at the head of the National Theatre. The New York critics gave him their Best Actor award (against competition from O'Toole, Brando, Lancaster and Mason) and the importance of *Sleuth* was, in Olivier's view, that it re-established him as a leading man in the cinema. It was also his first real non-classical screen success since leaving Hollywood in 1941.

At first, the elation of seeing Laurence Olivier in a starring role, after the merely tantalizing glimpses of him in recent roles, is sufficient to give *Sleuth* a high spirit. Olivier seems to be having a ripsnorting high old time in this show-off confection about an eccentric author of detective novels and his prey (Michael Caine) and he calls up memories of the giggly, boyish Olivier with the pencil moustache who used to dodge pursuing ladies in the thirties. But when the cleverness of Shaffer's excessive literacy wears down, and the stupid tricks the two men play on each other keep grinding on, with each in turn being humiliated, one begins to feel very uncomfortable that the greatest actor of our day — the man who must surely be the wittiest actor who has ever lived — is chasing around in the kind of third-rate material he outgrew more than thirty years ago. A friend in the theatre muttered, "It's Laurence Olivier playing a role that would have been perfect for George Sanders" . . . we may think that we could watch Olivier in anything and be ecstatically happy, but when the director is filling the void with repeated shots of mechanical toys grinning ominously we have plenty of time to experience the shame of being part of a culture that can finance Laurence Olivier only in a gentleman-bitch George Sanders role." — Pauline Kael, *New Yorker*

Among the toys, a moment of truth

MARATHON MAN

1976

Production company: Robert Evans and Sidney Beckerman for Paramount. *U.K. Release:* CIC. Panavision and Metrocolor. *Running time:* 126 minutes. *Producers:* Robert Evans and Sidney Beckerman. *Director:* John Schlesinger. *Associate producer:* George Justin. *Director of photography:* Conrad Hall, A.S.C. *Screenplay:* William Goldman, *from his novel. Production designer:* Richard MacDonald. *Music composed and conducted by:* Michael Small. *Edited by:* Jim Clark. *Art director:* Jack De Shields. *Assistant directors:* Howard W. Koch Jr., Burtt Harris. *Unit production manager:* Stephen F. Kesten. *Set decorator:* George Gaines. *Script supervisor:* Nick Sgarro. *Costumes:* Robert De Mora. *Make-up artist:* Ben Nye. *Hair stylist:* Barbara Lorenz. *Wardrobe:* Bernie Pollack, Robert M. Moore.

CAST

Dustin Hoffman	*Babe*
Laurence Olivier	*Szell*
Roy Scheider	*Doc*
William Devane	*Janaway*
Marthe Keller	*Elsa*
Fritz Weaver	*Professor Biesenthal*
Richard Bright	*Karl*
Marc Lawrence	*Erhard*
Allen Joseph	*Babe's Father*
Tito Goya	*Melendez*
Ben Dova	*Szell's Brother*
Lou Gilbert	*Rosenbaum*
Jacques	*LeClerc*
James Wing Woo	*Chen*
Nicole Deslauriers	*Nicole*
Lotta Andor-Palfi	*Old Lady on 47th Street*
Lionel Pina, Church, Tricoche, Jaime Tirelli, Wilfredo Hernandez	*Street Gang*
Harry Goz, Michael Vale, Fred Stuthman, Lee Steele	*Jewelry Salesmen*
William Martel	*Bank Guard*
Glenn Robards, Ric Carrott	*Plainclothesmen*
Alma Beltran	*Laundress*

STORY

The central figure is Babe (Dustin Hoffman), a New York history student obsessed both with the idea of becoming an Olympic marathon runner and with resentful memories of his father's suicide under the pressures of McCarthyist witch-hunts. His brother Doc (Roy Scheider), an American secret agent coming back from Europe, is promptly murdered by Szell (Laurence Olivier) an old Nazi who has returned from hiding in South America to retrieve a hidden hoard of diamonds, wartime loot from Jewish concentration-camp victims.

With Doc dead, Szell turns his attentions to Babe, suspecting that he is privy to some plot by Doc to snatch the fortune from him. Babe manages to escape from the tortures which Szell inflicts with a set of dentist's tools. From being a liberal pacifist, however, he is now transformed into a fiercely ag-

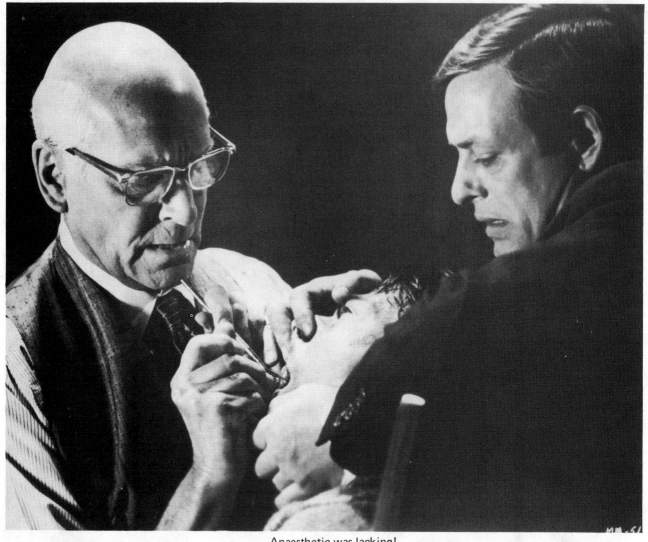

Anaesthetic was lacking!

gressive revenger and drives Szell to his death after preparing for him a much more exquisite torment, the sight of his treasure being irretrievably lost.

CRITICS' CIRCLE

"The official and pleasingly unpretentious description of John Schlesinger's new film is 'a thriller': technically this is apt, but surely too modest for a film which manages to comment interestingly on the activities of such spy organisations as the FBI and the CIA in America, the effects still being felt there of the McCarthy witch-hunt of communists in the 50s and the continuing presence of important Nazis hiding in South America . . . no film I can recall has seemed so likely, afterwards, to give rise to discussion and differences of opinion as to what happens, though none, I would say, on the quality of the acting and direction, especially in the choice of locations, nor on the daring of the narrative style which may be described as catch-it-if-you-can. Catch, at any rate, Olivier's performance

which hardly needed such an elaborate frame." — Patrick Gibbs, *Daily Telegraph*

"It is strongly played by Laurence Olivier (always at his best in roles that call for him to be seedy or nasty or both)." — David Robinson, *The Times*

"I know it is unfashionable today to confess to being shocked or disgusted in the theatre or cinema, and there are those who will hasten to explain — quite correctly as it happens — that *Marathon Man* is technically highly accomplished, and that it has been directed with flair and edited with skill. That is the whole trouble: if the sadism had been depicted ineptly, it would not have been half so disturbing." — Benny Green, *Punch*

"Olivier is one of the few who turn acting into one of the great humane professions of Western civilisation." — *Newsweek*

THE SEVEN-PER-CENT SOLUTION

1977

A Herbert Ross Film. *Released by:* Universal. *Distributed by:* CIC. Technicolor. *Country:* U.S. *Running time:* 114 minutes. *Producer and director:* Herbert Ross. *Executive producers:* Arlene Sellers and Alex Winitsky. *Associate producer:* Stanley O'Toole. *Director of photography:* Oswald Morris, B.S.C. *Screenplay:* Nicholas Meyer. *Production designed by:* Ken Adam. *Music:* John Addison. *'The Madame's Song' by:* Stephen Sondheim. *Editorial supervision by:* William Reynolds, A.C.E. *Costume designer:* Alan Barrett. *Assistant to Mr. Ross:* Nora Kaye. *Production associate:* Howard Jeffrey. *Production manager:* Michael Guest. *Continuity:* Ann Skinner. *Editor:* Chris Barnes. *Camera operators:* Jimmy Turrell, Mike Fox. *Art director:* Peter Lamont.

CAST

Alan Arkin . . . .*Sigmund Freud*
Vanessa Redgrave . . . . *Lola Deveraux*
Robert Duvall . . . .*Dr. Watson*
Nicol Williamson . . . . *Sherlock Holmes*
Laurence Olivier . . . . *Professor Moriarty*
Joel Grey. . . . .*Lowenstein*
Samantha Eggar. . . . . *Mary Watson*
Jeremy Kemp . . . . *Baron Von Leinsdorf*
Charles Gray . . . . *Mycroft Holmes*
Georgia Brown . . . . *Mrs. Freud*
Regine. . . . . *Madame*
Anna Quayle. . . . . *Freda*
Jill Townsend . . . . *Mrs. Holmes*
John Bird . . . . *Berger*
Alison Leggatt. . . . .*Mrs. Hudson*
Frederick Jaeger . . . . *Marker*
Erik Chitty . . . . *The Butler*
Jack May. . . . .*Dr. Schultz*
Gertan Klauber . . . .*The Pasha*
Leon Greene . . . . *Squire Holmes*
Michael Blagdon . . . . *Young Holmes*
Ashley House . . . . *Young Freud*
Sheila Shand Gibbs . . . . *Nun*
Erich Padalewsky . . . . *Station Master*
John Hill . . . . *Train Engineer*

STORY

In the Spring of 1891 Dr Watson finds Sherlock Holmes in his Baker Street flat, confused and agitated and talking of Moriarty, the "Napoleon of crime". Holmes is suffering from cocaine addiction and throws Watson out.

At his own home, Watson finds Professor Moriarty waiting for him. Moriarty tells him that Holmes has been following him, sending him threatening letters and telegrams and generally being a nuisance — slandering him everywhere. Moriarty explains that he was once Holmes's mathematics tutor and never did him any harm.

Watson, together with Sherlock's brother Mycroft, and Moriarty devise a complicated plan to lure Holmes to Vienna to be cured of his addiction by Dr Sigmund Freud.

After going through the drug withdrawal Holmes accompanies Freud on a visit to a former patient who has attempted suicide. She is Lola, a vibrant redhead who has actually been kidnapped by Baron Von Leinsdorf (whom Freud has just defeated in a mock duel — a game of tennis) and is about to be given to Amin Pasha. In exchange for her, the Pasha has agreed to pay the Baron's gambling debts.

After a mad railway chase and swordfight Lola is rescued. Freud discovers that Moriarty was the lover of Holmes's mother. When his father caught them he killed her and that was the reason for the fixation. Through deep hypnosis Freud removes it. Instead of going home to Baker Street Sherlock Holmes decides to take a holiday — with Lola.

CRITICS' CIRCLE

"The film is a civilized light entertainment — somewhere between the genial 'little' English comedies of the fifties, with their nifty plots and over-qualified performers, and the splashy stylized James Bond pictures. The director, Herbert Ross, works fluidly, serving the actors and the script unassumingly, and the designer, Ken Adam (who also did

the Bonds), has done the plush sets, stuffed to their Victorian gills. Movies don't often splurge on such a clever idea, and it's very pleasurable to see the casting and the details brought off without stinting . . . Olivier, who couldn't rise above the material in *Marathon Man*, is in tremendously high form. His Moriarty, a prissy complaining old pedagogue who feels persecuted by Holmes, is performed with the covert wit that is his specialty. It's not a big part, but this Moriarty — his face expressing injury to the verge of tears — is amusingly dislikable, a Dickensian monster." — Pauline Kael, *New Yorker*

"*The Seven-per-cent Solution* is two stories, neither one sturdy enough to support the weight of a full plot . . . The ace in this poorly shuffled deck (of

actors) is, no surprise, Olivier. He has not often done comedy on screen, but his extravagently funny Moriarty is a creation of wit and invention." — Jay Cocks, *Time*

"His Professor Moriarty is the most memorable feature in this curious combination of fact and fictitious fiction . . . As Holme's nemisis Moriarty, who may be just a figment of his drugged imagination or a memory from the past, Olivier gives a performance of majestically comic and alarming proportions." — Margaret Hinxman, *Daily Mail*

". . . the film is a profligate entertainment, in which much talent is gathered together only to be cast-off half-used . . . only Laurence Olivier as Moriarty manages to etch a distinctive character." — Geoff Porcion, *Financial Times*

A BRIDGE TOO FAR

1977

United Artists. *Country:* U.K. *Producers:* Joseph E. Levine, Richard P. Levine. *Director:* Richard Attenborough. *Co-producer:* Michael Stanley-Evans. *Screenplay by:* William Goldman, *from the book by:* Cornelius Ryan. *Music composed and conducted by:* John Addison. *Associate producer:* John Palmer. *Production supervisor:* Eric Rattray. *Production manager:* Terence Clegg. *Continuity:* Connie Willis. *Assistant director:* David Tomblin. *Director of photography:* Geoffrey Unsworth. *Camera operator:* Peter MacDonald. *Film editor:* Anthony Gibbs. *Sound:* Simon Kaye. *Production designer:* Terry Marsh. *Art directors:* Roy Stannard, Stuart Craig.

CAST

Dirk Bogarde . . . . *Lieut. General Frederick 'Boy' Browning*
James Caan . . . . *Staff Sergeant Eddie Dobun*
Michael Caine . . . . .*Lieut. Colonel 'Joe' Vandeleur*
Sean Connery . . . .*Major General Robert Urquhart*
Edward Fox . . . . . . *Lieut. General Brian Horrocks*
Elliott Gould . . . . *Colonel Bobby Stout*
Gene Hackman . . . .*Major General Stanislaw Sosabowski*
Anthony Hopkins . . . . . *Lieut. Colonel John Frost*
Hardy Kruger . . . . *General Ludwig*
Laurence Olivier . . . . *Dr. Spaander*
Ryan O'Neal . . . .*Brig. General James M. Gavin*
Robert Redford. . . . . *Major Julian Cook*
Maximilian Schell . . . . *Lieut. General Wilhelm Bittrich*
Liv Ullmann . . . . *Kate ter Horst*
Arthur Hill . . . . *Tough Colonel*
Wolfgang Preiss . . . .*Field Marshall Gerd Von Rundstedt*
Siem Vroom . . . . *Underground Leader*
Eric Van't Wout . . . .*Kid with Glasses*
Mary Smithuysen . . . .*Old Dutch Lady*
Marlies van Alcmaer . . . . *Wife*
Nicholas Campbell . . . . *Captain Glass*
Christopher Good . . . . *Major Carlyle*
Keith Drinkel . . . . *Lieut. Cornish*
Peter Faber . . . .*Captain Harry*

STORY

This is the enormous story of Operation Market Garden — a plan in September, 1944, to bring the war to a speedy end. It was formulated by Field-

Marshal Montgomery and sanctioned by General Eisenhower. Thirty-five thousand U.S. and British paratroops were to drop into Eastern Holland to secure the six major bridges leading to the German Border. Meanwhile, a formidable British ground force would speed up the 64-mile corridor from Belgium to the last bridge at Arnhem on the Rhine river. From Arnhem the combined allied armies would sweep right into the industrial Ruhr section of Germany and smash the already battered war production plants of the Third Reich. The plan, however, did not work due to a number of mistakes, misjudgements, bad luck and bad weather.

CRITICS' CIRCLE

". . . Whatever is lively and memorable in the film, which is not much, is provided by the English members of the most expensive all-star cast in recent memory . . . When events begin to overwhelm, director Attenborough loses his design in the smoke and din of a huge confused battle . . . Liv Ullmann and Laurence Olivier play long-suffering Dutch locals caught up in all this boom-boom in humble, long suffering style." · Richard Schickel, *Time*

". . . so muddled is the final impression left after nearly three hours by *A Bridge Too Far* based on Cornelius Ryan's account of the Arnhem operation in September 1944, and so curious the portraits given of several very senior British officers, that I can only assume something other was being attempted than a clear account of the battle . . . given the enormous scale of the production and the long list of stars and character actors, few seen to advantage, the result can only appear as a serious artistic misjudgement." — Patrick Gibbs, *Daily Telegraph*

". . . *A Bridge Too Far* is a reel too long. For another thing it is both confused and historically gap-toothed despite its legion of military and special advisers . . . Laurence Olivier and Liv Ullmann are given parts they could accomplish on their heads." — Derek Malcolm, *The Guardian*

". . . Laurence Olivier, as a Dutch doctor and Liv Ullmann, as a housewife might easily have phoned in their tiny parts . . . In this story any resemblance to persons living or dead is not coincidental — because the dead can't sue. This is the most expensive British film ever made and it looks it." — Bernard McElwaine, *Sunday Mirror*

"It is a film that tries well, wants to surmount any charge of sensationalism, but whose falling be-

190

With Liv Ullmann

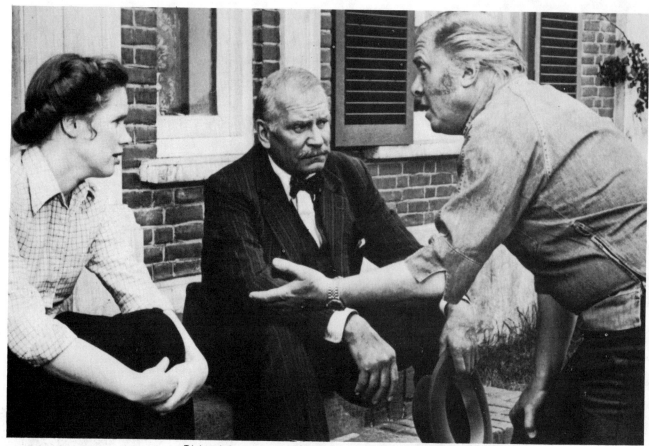

Richard Attenborough directs Olivier and Liv Ullmann

tween two stools results in its artistic collapse. It may deal in facts but, in the end, it does not result in any kind of statement of truth about men at war.'' — Tom Hutchinson, *Sunday Telegraph*

"Even so, it would be impossible for a film of this length and logistics not to have many moments, big and small, when the scale of it shakes you, the pity of it touches you. Such is the actual airdrop itself, a masterly piece of aerial photography with thousands of parachutes filling the sky till they look like cobbles in the clouds and the men could stand on the ones beneath them. Such is the desperate fording of the river by American troops in leaky boats, Robert Redford leading the paddling through watersheet of ammunition fire and a protective blanket of 'Hail Marys'. Such is the shy confession of one of our men that because he can't remember the password he always carries an umbrella into battle so as not to be taken for a German and the moment, too, when common humanity bridges the rival enmities and Laurence Olivier's Dutch doctor wins a cease-fire from the German commandant (Maximilian Schell) in order to bury the dead and surrender the wounded. . . . But when all's said and done and the last shot's been fired and the last note blown on the hunting horn that some over-eccentric British officer brings on to the field of war, *A Bridge Too Far* remains a curiously obsolescent exercise. I really doubt if one any longer wants movies that turn some horrifying human disaster into the stuff of visceral entertainment or try to celebrate the tens of thousands of unknowns who died and at the same time assign main roles to famous faces who glorify the Hollywood star system. *A Bridge Too Far* has a compromise too many for my comfort." — Alexander Walker, *Evening Standard*

Dr Spaander pleads with S.S. General Ludw

temporary truce to remove allied wounded

With producer Joseph E. Levine

Musing over a point with director Attenborough

With Anne Castaldini for the TV production of Ibsen's *John Gabriel Borkman*

OLIVIER: TELEVISION AND RADIO

In the course of a long and crowded career, Sir Laurence has made comparatively few radio broadcasts, though he has featured in the occasional play and of course broadcast on several state occasions, most notably perhaps the funerals of King George VI and Sir Winston Churchill.

On record, he once spoke a considerable part of the Old and New Testaments, and can also be found on many soundtrack recordings from his films as well as on albums of poetry and drama.

On television, he made his postwar acting debut in America in November 1958 as John Gabriel Borkman in the Ibsen play of that name, though there had been a prewar BBC *Macbeth* at Alexandra Palace. Then in 1959 he won an Emmy for "outstanding performance by an actor" as a result of his appearance in an NBC production of Maugham's *The Moon and Sixpence.*

In 1961 came his third appearance, this in the CBS production of Graham Greene's *The Power and the Glory*, full details of which will be found in the filmography since it was subsequently released within Europe as a film.

Then came television productions of two of Sir Laurence's National Theatre successes, both made in Britain by ATV: *The Merchant of Venice* (1972) and *Long Day's Journey Into Night* (1973) for which Sir Laurence won his second Emmy.

Sir Laurence has also voiced numerous television documentaries, most notably the Thames Television *World At War* series, and in 1974 he was also to be seen, though on American television only, advertising Polaroid cameras.

Early in 1974 it had been thought that Sir Laurence would take over from Rex Harrison the title rôle in a screen version of John Mortimer's *A Voyage*

The pound of flesh! Opposite Joan Plowright in *Merchant of Venice*

Round My Father but filming was abruptly halted due to economic difficulties.

Later that year, Olivier appeared (for the first time) opposite Katharine Hepburn in a television film of Angela Thirkell's novel *Love Among The Ruins*. The director (for ABCtv in America) was George Cukor and the cast also included Colin Blakely, Joan Sims and Richard Pearson. It premiered in New York in March 1975 and was shown on BBC television over Christmas 1976. Also in that year came his Nicodemus in the epic six-hour *Jesus of Nazareth* directed by Franco Zeffirelli, and shown on television over Easter 1977.

In the meantime Sir Laurence had joined Granada Television (at the invitation of his brother-in-law David Plowright) to arrange, produce and sometimes also direct and star in a series called "The Best Play of the Year". He himself had the choice of plays, of which the first three were:

THE COLLECTION
by Harold Pinter

Alan Bates	*James*
Malcolm McDowell	*Bill*
Helen Mirren	*Stella*
Laurence Olivier	*Harry*

Designer: Michael Grimes. *Producers:* Laurence Olivier, Derek Granger. *Director:* Michael Apted. *Transmission:* Sunday, 5 December 1976.

CAT ON A HOT TIN ROOF
by Tennessee Williams

Natalie Wood	*Maggie*
Robert Wagner	*Brick*
Maureen Stapleton	*Big Mama*
Laurence Olivier	*Big Daddy*
Mary Peach	*Mae*
Jack Hedley	*Gooper*
David Healey	*Dr Baugh*

Designer: Peter Phillips. *Producers:* Derek Granger, Laurence Olivier. *Director:* Robert Moore. *Transmission:* Sunday, 12 December 1976.

HINDLE WAKES
by Stanley Houghton

Jack Hedley	*Christopher Hawthorn*
Rosemary Leach	*Mrs Hawthorn*
Rosalind Ayres	*Fanny Hawthorn*
Donald Pleasence	*Nathanial Jeffcote*
Pat Heywood	*Mrs Jeffcote*
Trevor Eve	*Alan Jeffcote*
Roy Dotrice	*Sir Timothy Farrer*

From *Long Day's Journey Into Night*

Judi Bowker . . . .*Beatrice Farrer*
Designer: Alan Price. *Produced and directed by:*
Laurence Olivier and June Howson. *Transmission:*
Sunday, 19 December 1976.

Asked at this time why he had gone into television
so determinedly, Sir Laurence replied, "I stood
aloof from it for far too long; now I realise I live in
the television age and I must just get on with it."
Early in 1977 he started work on the fourth of
these Granada "specials", *Come Back Little Sheba*
which he co-produced with Derek Granger. Silvio
Narizzano directed a cast headed by Olivier,
Joanne Woodward, Patience Collier and Carrie
Fisher and as with the previous productions NBC
were the American television company involved.
Future productions in this series are unconfirmed
at the time of going to press, but are likely to in-
clude Bridie's *Daphne Laureola* (with Joan Plowright in the lead), *Saturday, Sunday, Monday*, and
Osborne's *A Patriot For Me*. "This entire series"
said the *Los Angeles Times* in January 1977 "may
be one of the best reasons to own a television set".

Long Day's Journey Into Night

As Big Daddy, the self-made millionaire in Tennessee Williams's *Cat on A Hot Tin Roof*

As Harry Kane, a rich, ageing homosexual dress designer, in Harold Pinter's *The Collection*

JESUS OF NAZARETH

An ATV/RAI co-production for television and the cinema. *Country:* U.K. *Producer:* Vincenzo Labella. *Director:* Franco Zeffirelli. *Screenplay:* Anthony Burgess and Suso Cecchi d'Amico.

CAST
Robert Powell . . . .*Jesus*
Olivia Hussey. . . . .*Mary*
James Mason . . . . *Joseph of Arimathea*
Laurence Olivier . . . .*Nicodemus*
Ernest Borgnine. . . . . *The Centurion*
Peter Ustinov. . . . .*Herod*
Ralph Richardson . . . .*Simeon*
Rod Steiger . . . .*Pontius Pilate*
Donald Pleasence. . . . .*Melchior*
Michael York. . . . .*John the Baptist*
Claudia Cardinale . . . .*The Adulteress*
Christopher Plummer . . . .*Herod Antipas*

Robert Powell as Jesus

Peter Ustinov as Herod

Ian McShane as Judas Iscariot

Rod Steiger as Pontius
Pilate

Olivier as Nicodemus

With Joanne Woodward, Olivier's co-star in *Come Back Little Sheba*

OLIVIER: STAGE CHRONOLOGY

1922 — April: Shakespeare Festival Theatre, Stratford-upon-Avon (special boys' performance), Katharina in *The Taming Of The Shrew*.

1924 — November: Century Theatre, the Suliot Officer in *Byron*.

1925 — February: Regent Theatre, Thomas of Clarence and Snare in *King Henry IV part 2*.

1925 — Summer: Brighton Hippodrome company.

1925 — December: Empire Theatre, *Henry VIII* and *The Cenci*.

1926 to 1928: Birmingham Repertory Company.

1926 — April: Kingsway Theatre, Minstrel in *The Marvellous History of St. Bernard*.

1926 — July: Touring, Richard Croaker in *The Farmer's Wife*.

1928 — January to April: appeared with the Birmingham company at the Royal Court in London: The Young Man in *The Adding Machine*; Malcolm in *Macbeth*; Martellus in *Back To Methuselah*; Harold in *Harold*; The Lord in *The Taming Of The Shrew*.

1928 — June: Royalty Theatre, Gerald Arnwood in *Bird In Hand*.

1928 — December. Apollo Theatre, Captain Stanhope in *Journey's End*.

1929 — January: His Majesty's Theatre, Michael (Beau) Geste in *Beau Geste*.

1929 — March: New Theatre, Prince Po in *The Circle Of Chalk*.

1929 — April: Lyric Theatre, Richard Parish in *Paris Bound*.

1929 — August: Eltinge Theatre, New York, Hugh Bromilow in *Murder On The Second Floor*.

1929 — December: Fortune Theatre, Jerry Warrender in *The Lost Enemy*.

1930 — March: Arts Theatre, Ralph in *After All*.

1930 — September: Phoenix Theatre, Victor Prynne in *Private Lives*.

1931 — January: Times Square Theatre, New York, Victor Prynne in *Private Lives*.

1933 — April: Playhouse, Steven Beringer in *The Rats of Norway*.

1933 — April: Playhouse, Steven Beringer in *The Dulcimer in The Green Bay Tree*.

1934 — April: Globe Theatre, Richard Kurt in *Biography*.

1934 — June: New Theatre, Bothwell in *Queen Of Scots*.

1934 — October: Lyric Theatre, Anthony Cavendish in *Theatre Royal*.

1935 — March: Shaftesbury Theatre, Peter Hammond in *Ringmaster*.

1935 — May: Whitehall Theatre, Richard Harben in *Golden Arrow*.

1935 — October: New Theatre, Romeo in *Romeo And Juliet*.

1935 — November: New Theatre, Mercutio in *Romeo and Juliet*.

1936 — May: Lyric Theatre, Robert Patch in *Bees On The Boat Deck*

1937 — January to November: Old Vic: Hamlet in *Hamlet*; Sir Toby Belch in *Twelfth Night*; King Henry in *Henry V*; Macbeth in *Macbeth*.

1937 — June: Kronborg Castle, Elsinore, *Hamlet*.

1937 — December: New Theatre, *Macbeth*.

1938 — February to April: Old Vic: Iago in *Othello*; Vivaldi in *The King Of Nowhere*; Caius Marcius in *Coriolanus*.

1939 — April: Ethel Barrymore Theatre, New York, Gaylord Easterbrook in *No Time For Comedy*.

1940 — May, 51st Street Theatre, New York, Romeo in *Romeo And Juliet* (directed).

1944 — August: New Theatre (Old Vic company): Button Moulder in *Peer Gynt*; Sergius Saranoff in *Arms And The Man*; Duke of Gloucester in *Richard III*; Astrov in *Uncle Vanya*.

1945-1946 — Old Vic: Hotspur in *Henry IV (part 1)*; Justice Shallow in *Henry IV (part 2)*; Oedipus in *Oedipus Rex*;

Puff in *The Critic;*
King Lear.
1945 — July: Comédie Française:
Peer Gynt;
Arms And The Man;
Richard III.
1946 — May: Century Theatre, New York, Oedipus, Puff, Button Moulder, Saranoff, Richard.
1946 — September: New Theatre (Old Vic Company), *King Lear* (directed).
1948 — February: Toured Australia and New Zealand with the Old Vic Company:
Sir Peter Teazle in *The School For Scandal;*
Richard III;
Mr Antrobus in *The Skin Of Our Teeth.*
1949 — January to February: New Theatre (Old Vic Company):
Richard III;
Sir Peter Teazle in *The School For Scandal;*
(directed);
Chorus in *Antigone* (directed);
also directed *The Proposal.*
1950 — January: St James's Theatre:
Caesar in *Caesar And Cleopatra;*
Antony in *Antony And Cleopatra.*
1951 — December: Ziegfield, New York:
Caesar in *Caesar And Cleopatra;*
Antony in *Caesar And Cleopatra.*
1952 — February: New Century Theatre, New York, *Venus Observed* (directed).
1953 — November: Phoenix Theatre, Grand Duke in *The Sleeping Prince.*
1955 — Shakespeare Memorial Theatre, Stratford:
Macbeth;
Titus Andronicus;
Malvolio in *Twelfth Night.*
1957 — April: Royal Court Theatre, Archie Rice in *The Entertainer.*
1957 — Toured Europe in *Titus Andronicus.* Played in Paris, Venice, Belgrade, Zagreb, Vienna and Warsaw.
1957 — September: Palace Theatre, Archie Rice in *The Entertainer.*
1958 — February: Royale Theatre, New York, Archie Rice in *The Entertainer.*
1959 — July: Shakespeare Memorial Theatre, Stratford, *Coriolanus.*
1960 — April: Royal Court theatre, Berenger in *Rhinoceros.*
1960 — July: Strand Theatre, Berenger in *Rhinoceros.*
1960 — October: St James's Theatre, Becket in *Becket.*
1961 — March: Toured, Henry II in *Becket.*
1961 — May: Hudson Theatre, New York, *Becket.*
1962 — July: Chichester Festival Theatre:

The Chances (directed);
The Prologue and Bassanes in *The Broken Heart* (directed);
Astrov in *Uncle Vanya* (directed);
1962 — Saville Theatre, Fred Midway in *Semi-Detached.*
1963 — July: Chichester Festival Theatre, Astrov in *Uncle Vanya* (directed).
1963 — October: Old Vic Theatre, (National Theatre Company):
Hamlet (directed);
Astrov in *Uncle Vanya* (directed);
Captain Brazen in *The Recruiting Officer.*
1964 — Old Vic Theatre (National Theatre Company):
Othello;
Halvard Solness in *The Master Builder.*
1965 — Old Vic Theatre (National Theatre Company), *The Crucible* (directed).
1965 — September: Toured Moscow and Berlin with the National Theatre company:
Othello in *Othello;*
Tattle in *Love For Love.*
1965 — October: Old Vic Theatre, Tattle in *Love For Love.*
1966 — Old Vic Theatre (National Theatre Company):
Juno And The Paycock (directed);
The Crucible (directed).
1967 — Old Vic Theatre (National Theatre Company):
Edgar in *The Dance Of Death;*
Three Sisters (directed).
1967 — Toured Canada with the National Theatre Company:
Love For Love;
The Dance Of Death;
Plucheux in *A Flea In Her Ear.*
1968 — Old Vic Theatre (National Theatre Company):
The Advertisement (co-directed);
Love's Labour's Lost (directed).
1969 — Old Vic Theatre (National Theatre Company):
A. B. Raham in *Home And Beauty;*
Three Sisters (directed).
1970 — Old Vic Theatre (National Theatre Company), Shylock in *The Merchant Of Venice.*
1971 — Old Vic Theatre (National Theatre Company), James Tyrone in *Long Day's Journey Into Night.*
1973 — Old Vic Theatre (National Theatre Company):
Antonio in *Saturday, Sunday, Monday;*
John Tagg in *The Party.*
1974 — Old Vic Theatre (National Theatre Company), *Eden End* (directed).

Salvador Dali's Olivier

OLIVIER: BIBLIOGRAPHY.

The authors would like to acknowledge their gratitude to the many critics, reporters, authors and publishers whose work has been consulted and quoted in the text. The following is a selective rather than exhaustive list of those books which may prove most useful to any student of Olivier's career in the cinema:

AGEE ON FILM: James Agee (*Peter Owen, London, 1967*); BRITISH FILM YEAR BOOKS: Peter Noble (ed) (*Skelton Robinson, London, 1948-50*); CRY GOD FOR LARRY: Virginia Fairweather (*Calder & Boyars, London, 1969*); THE FILM *HAMLET*: Brenda Cross (ed) (*Saturn Press, London, 1948*); FOCUS ON SHAKESPEARIAN FILMS: Charles Eckert (ed) (*Prentice-Hall, U.S., 1972*); GREAT MOVIE STARS: THE GOLDEN YEARS: David Shipman (*Hamlyn, London, 1970*); *HAMLET* THE FILM AND THE PLAY: Alan Dent (*World Film Publishing, London, 1948*); LAURENCE OLIVIER: W.A. Darlington (*Morgan Grampian, London, 1968*); LAURENCE OLIVIER: John Cottrell (*Weidenfeld & Nicolson, London, 1975*); OLIVIER: Logan Gourlay (ed) (*Weidenfeld & Nicolson, London, 1973*); THE OLIVIERS: Felix Barker (*Hamish Hamilton, London, 1953*); SHAKESPEARE AND THE FILM: Roger Manvell (*Dent, London, 1971*).